Praise for
Faith in the Flames

Faith in the Flames: Transforming Hope and Healing offers a compelling exploration of the complex interplay between dreams, expectations, and reality. While acknowledging the pain and disappointment that often accompany unmet aspirations, Shawna ultimately provides a message of hope and resilience, encouraging readers to find strength in faith, shared experiences, and the potential for growth through adversity.

Michael S. Miller, author of *Maci's Place* and *Strong Finish*

The belief is that if you are a Christian, your life is wrapped up perfectly in a bow. But as believers, we know that is far from the truth. It is through life challenges that we see God, feel God, and trust that *His* plan has been perfectly designed for us. Reading this, you will feel His presence through Shawna's vulnerability, strength, and faithfulness in her journey. Being a mama isn't easy, but being a child of God gives us comfort and hope.

Kimberly Cabral, founder of MASK (Mothers Awareness on School-Aged Kids)

Shawna provides a beacon of light that helps all of us appreciate and embrace our true power within and our connection with God. Every one of us experiences events that tip our world upside down, and it is how we respond that defines us. Shawna gives us hope and insight into how we can all shift from being overwhelmed to taking back control of our lives. She guides us on our journey as we deal with the initial trauma and shock and on through the acceptance of a new reality, where we again become creators of the lives we deserve. She emboldens us to be brave, to recognize that through adversity, we discover new strengths and that we grow spiritually. We learn how to love and be compassionate in ways we never imagined, bringing us closer to godliness and new beginnings.

Charlie McCready, parental alienation coach, illuminating the way for parents to bring they and their children out of the darkness of alienation

Shawna's *Faith in the Flames* is more than just a book about overcoming trauma; it's a lifeline for anyone who has experienced the profound pain of loss, whether it be the loss of a child, a relationship, a dream, or even a part of themselves. As someone who has a deep understanding of the devastating impact of parental alienation, I can attest to the power of Shawna's words. Her book offers a roadmap for navigating grief, finding strength in adversity, and, ultimately, discovering meaning in the midst of pain. Shawna's writing style is warm, encouraging, and deeply personal, like having a conversation with a trusted friend. She doesn't shy away from difficult emotions but offers a beacon of hope, reminding us that even in the darkest of times, there is always a path to healing and restoration. I wholeheartedly recommend *Faith in the Flames* to anyone seeking to move forward from trauma, embrace their new reality, and find joy and purpose in their life. Shawna's words have the power to transform hearts and guide us towards a brighter future.

Amanda Sillars, BpsycSc, founder of Eeny Meeny Miney Mo Foundation, advocacy and psychoeducation in parent-child trauma, coerced attachment and alienation

Shawna sheds light on the heartbreaking issue of parental alienation, revealing its profound emotional toll on children and families. With wisdom, clarity, and a heart for healing, *Faith in the Flames* not only explains the complexities of alienation but also offers hope through actionable steps toward forgiveness. This book serves as a powerful reminder that through God's grace, even the most fractured relationships can find a path to healing.

Dr. Don Wilson, founding pastor of Christ's Church of the Valley

With raw honesty, Shawna shares her beautiful testament to God's ability to turn our deepest wounds into powerful purposes. Facing the unthinkable loss of children who are still living and navigating this unique grief, she endured a nearly unimaginable pain. Yet, through her incredible faith journey, she reveals how God can carry us and strengthen us through the most heartbreaking of circumstances. Shawna's story is heart-wrenching and brave, and it shines a light on a type of trauma many people silently endure. Her journey will resonate deeply with anyone who has faced unspeakable pain or loss. But more than just a personal story, this book is a guide for turning tragedy into triumph, and also a comfort of how God faithfully leads us through what we can't face alone. In *Faith in the Flames: Transforming Trauma into Hope and Healing*, Shawna offers readers not only compassion and support but also a path forward—a way to find faith, healing, and, most of all, renewed hope.

Tierney Shirrell, Christian business coach, Live Bold founder, event host, speaker, podcaster, 2X best-selling author

Faith in the Flames by Shawna Foster provides a glimpse into a faith-based journey comprised of the greatest pains and most triumphant joy, guided by a loving God. Immerse yourself as if you're sitting by a fire on a snowy night in a room filled with cozy blankets, sipping a glass of wine or hot chocolate with a friend. This heartfelt, honest "share" filled with vulnerability, hard truths, and healing promises addresses the universal needs of those experiencing loss of love, hopes, and dreams, who must replace them with new meaningful paths and the ability to thrive and impact others positively. From the perspective of a loving mother's heart, Shawna shares how to step out in faith with courage and confidence, filled with scripturally relevant reminders of God's path and promises, which brings to mind one of my favorite verses for difficult moments: Isaiah 43:19. Shawna ultimately leads you toward practical solutions from heartfelt personal experience, and a glimpse into the possibility of *rejoicing* in *triumph* over evil, with a peace that surpasses understanding. "People who have gone through the DARKEST of trauma and pain and find the strength to endure, survive, and thrive, instead of allowing the pain to destroy them, become some of the most 'soulful' and deeply empathetic people I have ever known, with the capacity to impact lives in a way that *cascades down through generations.*"

Bryan Hale, coach for attachment trauma/dysfunction ("parental alienation") and various life goal areas, dad, bilingual Internationally certified hiking/excursion guide (both literally and figuratively, conquering "Summits")

Shawna's testimony in *Faith in the Flames* is an honest reflection of the pain and turmoil families face during challenging times, but also a hopeful vision for healing and renewal. This book is a beacon of hope for those navigating the stormy seas of family challenges, offering encouragement for finding peace amid turmoil. It is a must-read for anyone seeking to rebuild, strengthen, and restore their family relationships through God's love and guidance.

Pastor Tommy Barnett, co-Pastor Dream City Church Phoenix

FAITH
in the
FLAMES

Transforming Trauma into Hope and Healing

SHAWNA MARIE
FOSTER

Faith in the Flames: Transforming Trauma into Hope
Virginia Beach, VA
Copyright 2025 © Shawna Marie Foster
ISBN (paperback): 978-1-7379022-5-6

> **Disclaimer:** The author's opinions expressed herein are based on her personal experiences, observations, and readings on the subject matter. The author's opinions may not be universally applicable to all people in all circumstances. The information presented in this book is in no way intended as a substitute for legal, spiritual, medical, psychological, or other counseling. The author makes no representations or warranties, express or implied, about the completeness, accuracy, reliability, suitability or availability with respect to the information contained in this book for any purpose. The author of this book disclaims liability for any loss or damage suffered by any person as a result of the contents of this book.

Copyright © 2025 by Shawna Foster

All rights reserved. Unauthorized duplication is a violation of applicable law. No part of this publication may be reproduced or transmitted in any form or by any means. Electronic or mechanical, including photocopy, recording, or any information storage and retrieval system, without the express written permission of the author (except by a reviewer, who may quote brief passages and/or display brief passages in a short video clip, as a part of a professional review).

Unless otherwise marked, scriptures taken from the Holy Bible, New International Version®, NIV®. Copyright © 1973, 1978, 1984, 2011 by Biblica, Inc.™ Used by permission of Zondervan. All rights reserved worldwide. www.zondervan.com. The "NIV" and "New International Version" are trademarks registered in the United States Patent and Trademark Office by Biblica, Inc.™

Scripture quotations marked KJV taken from The King James Version, public domain.

Scripture quotations marked ESV are from The ESV® Bible (The Holy Bible, English Standard Version®), © 2001 by Crossway, a publishing ministry of Good News Publishers. Used by permission. All rights reserved.

Scripture quotations marked NLT are taken from the *Holy Bible*, New Living Translation, Copyright © 1996, 2004, 2015 by Tyndale House Foundation. Used by permission of Tyndale House Publishers, Inc., Carol Stream, Illinois 60188. All rights reserved.

Published by F.I.T. Press

THIS BOOK IS DEDICATED TO…

those who are hurting beyond measure and surviving more than you ever thought you were capable of enduring. It is my prayer that the words within these pages meet you exactly where you are, that they help you know that you are not alone. You are not meant to stay stuck in suffering. I want to help you find hope in this place. To remind you that you have a purpose – and that you are so very loved.

Table of Contents

Acknowledgments xiii
Preface xvii
INTRODUCTION | Battle Cry 1
CHAPTER ONE | The Plan—Not 7
CHAPTER TWO | From Dust to Dust 23
CHAPTER THREE | Anchor of Hope 37
CHAPTER FOUR | I Need a Minute 49
CHAPTER FIVE | Tearing Down the Walls 65
CHAPTER SIX | Renewed in the Ruins 79
CHAPTER SEVEN | In the Arms of My Refuge 93
CHAPTER EIGHT | Waiting Room 107
CHAPTER NINE | Forgiving the Unforgivable 123
CHAPTER TEN | Beyond the Rearview 139
CHAPTER ELEVEN | Harvesting Joy 157
CHAPTER TWELVE | Naked and Afraid 169
CHAPTER THIRTEEN | Sound the Trumpets 181
Afterword 189
About the Author 191
Next Steps 193

Acknowledgments

A very special thank you to my patient and strong husband. Dylan. I am so grateful for your love and your support. And thank you for stopping every time I come to you and say, "Will you hold me?" Your perfect hugs bring me so much peace and comfort. You didn't have to endure it all, but you did. Every moment, you still chose me, even through a battle that wasn't yours to suffer. Thank you for loving me. Thank you for believing in me and always supporting me in every project I start, especially this one. Thank you for dreaming with me.

Boy 2, your love, your phone calls and messages, and your constant smile bring me so much joy. I am honored to be your mama and to be loved by you. Thank you for choosing me.

To all three of my children, you are all I ever wanted. I love you always and forever and no matter what. —Forever, your mama.

To my mom and dad, you have been beside me always. Thank you for having my back and not turning against me in the crazy. Thank you for the laughs amid the tears, and always listening ears. And to the rest of my family, ditto!

Angie . . . wow! What a life it's been! I am so grateful for you. Thank you for always loving me. For always supporting me in everything I do. For always being my constant. When I prayed for you, I had no idea how big of a job it would be for you. In every way, you have done more than I asked for.

Jana, thank you for your constant check-ins, your unconditional love, and your support. I know we were brought together to do this crazy life together.

Judy, thank you for managing me, loving me, bringing me caffeine and chocolate, and for protecting my "minute" when I was hiding under my desk. You stood in the crazy with me most days, and I am forever grateful for you.

To my amazing friends, it would take a whole chapter to name you all. Thank you. You mean the world to me. Thank you for knowing who I am, lifting me up, and always showing me I'm not alone. Thank you for the laughs and adventures and beautiful memories.

To the beautiful communities of women that I know God handpicked just for me, thank you for loving me, lifting me up, supporting me, and encouraging me to step out boldly in faith and to be obedient to what God was asking me to do. Thank you for the safe space you have given me to practice vulnerability and for showing me how the enemy is a liar. Thank you for your constant prayers over me and this project.

To Fit Press and my amazing team, thank you for your faith in me and for giving me the tools to make this possible, for making this calling a reality, and for helping me bring hope to so many. Candice, thank you for prayerfully standing with me in every crazy thing that popped up. Thank you, especially, for your coaching and calming in the chaos. Tamra, your beautiful light is such a special piece to this project. Thank you for standing with me in my message and locking arms with me to love on as many as I can. Cortney, a special thank you for taking my words and polishing them up to make sure my readers would truly know and feel the message I wanted to share.

ACKNOWLEDGMENTS

To you, my readers, thank you for being here with me and allowing me to share the journey through my brokenness and into hope and healing. Thank you for allowing me to speak into your hearts. Friends, together, we've got this!

And most of all, thank you to my loving Heavenly Father. Thank you for carrying me every second of my heartbreak. For your loving arms wrapped around me. For healing me. Thank you for the beautiful people you have brought into my life. Thank you for blessing me with this incredible opportunity to share *You* with others and pour into those who are hurting—and your constant reminders to keep going. Thank you for leading the way and meeting me with an answer to every concern I brought to you. Thank you for your constant direction. Thank you for reminding me of who *You* say I am.

Preface

Healing is not supposed to be ever-seeking and never-finding. God is teaching me to find happiness and joy right where I am. I am blessed to do life with family and friends who love me and support me unconditionally, including a faithful husband who has walked through the flames with me, and my precious son, whom I'll affectionately call Boy 2 within these pages, who shows me every day who God says I am. I am so very grateful for these people and the moments I get to share with them. Through the suffering I've endured, I am learning to live my best life and find gratitude for what is versus what I had hoped my life would look like.

God asked me to write this book for you, beautiful friend. To help you in your time of brokenness. And to share with you how He brought me through what I could never have survived on my own. To share with you my mama heart, my healing, and my hope. As I wrestled with God about which details He was asking me to share with you (before I stepped aside and allowed Him to pour Himself out onto these pages), I took every attack from the enemy straight to Him. And in every lie from the enemy, God gave me the truthful answers my heart needed so He could speak directly to you here.

The pages of this book are not where you'll read the unbelievable details of what happened in my journey that caused me to have my heart ripped from my chest and be crushed to dust, bringing on every ugly cry, every panic, and every sleepless, tear-filled night. What you will find in our vulnerable time together is the understanding that even though our suffering may be different, you are not alone. I am here to walk with you.

Friend, as we journey through these pages together, know this is God's story. This is His promise to you, beautiful child of His. He knows your hurt. He knows your suffering. The illnesses that have come in your heartbreak. All of your losses. He knows every tear. Every painful moment that you've endured. He's asking you, right here and right now, not to stay rooted in your suffering. He's asking you to take His hand and let Him pull you out of the flames. He wants to meet you exactly where you are, right here. To erase the horrible replays in your mind. To help you forgive yourself and others. To heal. To show you who He says you are. To dry your tears and soften the sorrow you feel in your soul. To bring you through the thing that you never thought you could survive. To dream again. To mold your broken pieces into a new and beautiful creation. To give you a new hope. And a new purpose. To make you new through and through!

There is a time for everything,

and a season for every activity under the heavens:
a time to be born and a time to die,
a time to plant and a time to uproot,
a time to kill and a time to heal,
a time to tear down and a time to build,
a time to weep and a time to laugh,
a time to mourn and a time to dance,
a time to scatter stones and a time to gather them,
a time to embrace and a time to refrain from embracing,
a time to search and a time to give up,
a time to keep and a time to throw away,
a time to tear and a time to mend,
a time to be silent and a time to speak,
a time to love and a time to hate,
a time for war and a time for peace.

Ecclesiastes 3:1-8

Introduction

Battle Cry

Some moments change our lives completely, making certain that from that point forward, nothing is ever the same again. These moments divide our lives into "before" and "after."

We have beautiful, expected moments that divide our lives, such as wedding days, the births of children, and buying perfect homes. We also have events that alter life into a before and after that are historical, affecting most of the world, like wars, natural disasters, and traumatic events.

And then, there are the unexpected and tragic personal events that happen, which also create a before and after. Those moments we don't plan for or want. The moments that crush us to dust in an instant. It is in these that we know life will never be the way it was, for a moment much greater in significance than the ending of a normal chapter or a short season has occurred. It's larger. More impactful. More life-altering. And way more painful. It's not the end of our stories, but it's a definite end to a large part of them. It's often a complete shift in direction.

This moment of life's before and after may be caused by an unexpected accident or disease. Maybe it comes in the form of divorce or betrayal. It could be the ending of a lifelong career or a special friendship. The super scary event of a natural disaster or home invasion. Or maybe it's the loss of a child due to death, illness, abduction, addiction, overdose, miscarriage, estrangement, or alienation. The moment that creates a stop in time and lays the foundation of our before and after is something so significant that there is no way life after that moment will ever be the same — it becomes something far from what it was before.

On a beautiful day in mid-December, a day that was supposed to be a day of celebration and accomplishment, a day when I could finally witness so much of my hard work pay off and rejoice in my labors, I experienced one of these shifts. I had spent countless hours of class and study time preparing to take my real estate exam and get licensed. Instead of celebrating, my entire world changed. My heart was brutally ripped from my chest through a handwritten note left by my oldest son, crumpled up and lying all alone on my kitchen counter. The note told me that, in any way possible, I would not see him again.

I was about to be on the front lines of the biggest battle of my life. Shock and fear overtook me. I stood in unbelief, unable to move, staring blankly into the space of my empty living room. The next section of my book called Life now read, "Unimaginable Horror." The beautiful life I was living and all my expectations for the future had changed in an instant. My life would never look the same again.

> The next section of my book called Life now read, "Unimaginable Horror."

The Holy Spirit told me to pick up my purse and keys and go, to stop for a coffee on the way, and to still take the real estate exam because I wouldn't have the capacity to succeed at passing the test later. This was my only shot. And the Holy Spirit was right. Two weeks later, still in shock, drowning in fear and tears, and suffocating in the unimaginable heartbreak of my mama heart, it happened again. What broken pieces remained were further shattered to dust because, this time, it was my daughter who was to leave a note and say goodbye.

In an instant, everything changed — again.

Life had been exceptional in the many months leading up to this double devastation. All that had been rocky in previous years had seemed to calm down. The kids were doing great. Dylan, my husband, and I were awesome. Our business was growing — finally thriving after years of long hours and hard work. We could spend our evenings and weekends with the kids, supporting them in their athletics and activities, and on the occasion we didn't have sporting events, we were gone for the weekend exploring, having adventures, and making memories. When the kids were with their dad, Dylan and I would take trips, making private memories of our own. After some tumultuous years, I felt like I could smile and laugh again. There was a lot of joy and fun leading up to the days that changed our lives as we knew it.

I didn't know this loss was coming. It was like being hit by a silent runaway freight train, slamming into me and crushing me. There were no horns or screeching brakes to warn me of the blunt impact, the coming trauma. It stole every breath I had. Every part of me was shattered. The pain was the worst pain I'd ever experienced.

The world around me seemed to spin, and it all felt so weird. Eerie. Like the events taking place weren't even real. Still, to this day, the only term I can come up with to describe this period is to call it *The Twilight Zone*. I felt like I was living in an episode. I could even hear the soundtrack playing in the background of my mind. And I could picture myself as a little girl, standing in the front seat of the family's truck with my dad, as he drove up the skinniest dirt road I'd ever seen, winding back and forth up the mountainside to my grandpa's cabin. It was darker than dark. My dad looked at me and said, "Do you want to see something really scary?" (He was reciting *The Twilight Zone*.)

Nope. No, I don't. No thanks. I'll take this one as a pass, please!

I imagine the same is true for your before-and-after story. You just wish you could have passed it by.

I also didn't fully understand what "it" was that was happening. I didn't even know this type of abandonment was possible. How could I go from a beautiful and close relationship with all of my children, snuggling on the couch with them, receiving unexpected loving acts of service from them, enjoying their long hugs and I love yous, being involved in every aspect of their lives, or sitting around the kitchen table laughing and playing games with them in the days and moments just before? Only to have these beautiful daily moments become just memories in my next breath . . . to have the most recent family photos be the last with all of us together? And to not even know it was coming. The last vacation. The last camping trip. The last . . . everything. All that was left were just beautiful and amazing memories, which I grip onto with white knuckles even to this day.

I had never heard the term or words before that soon would be used to describe me. They would become a part of my regular vocabulary. I didn't know I'd be receiving a new "I am," one that I didn't want or deserve. I didn't know there was a list of signs or techniques to watch out for that would create this Hell I was being violently shoved into. I couldn't even fathom how in the world this could all be possible. And even more specifically, how could this happen to me? To us?

I suffer the loss of two children who are still living. I am a mama who lost two of my children because of *parental alienation (PA)*. Psychology Today defines parental alienation as when a child refuses to have a relationship with a parent because of manipulation, usually done as exaggerated or false information presented by the other parent.

This didn't have to happen. PA is traumatic and tragic to the children, the alienated parent, and the alienated extended family, often causing emotional issues for the child(ren), including long-term psychological effects, mental health disorders, self-destructive behaviors, suicidal ideation, and a lack of impulse control, to name a few. PA is a horrific form of mental abuse, and I pray that with continued exposure and awareness, other children and parents won't have to endure this kind of preventable trauma and suffering.

> God gave me the "I am" of mama. He did not give me this new "I am" of an alienated parent.

God gave me the "I am" of mama. He did not give me this new "I am" of an alienated parent. But friend, He makes us a promise, you and me—everyone. He promises He will use all things for good. Even this. Even this "I am" part of me, which I never asked for or earned, is an excruciating, life-changing part of my story. He can make it good too. I now know this "I am" is not *who* I am, and neither is it my entire story. And friend, the painfully messy part of your story, it's not who you are, either.

Losing two of my children has been the most horrific, painful, heartbreaking, *all-of-my-being-destroying* thing I've ever been forced to endure. (And I had endured much to this point in my life, but that's a conversation for another day.) In addition to having two of my children taken from me, I entered a hard war, one filled with battles—costing many tens of thousands of dollars—

including fighting for them, fighting the false accusations, fighting for my youngest son, who had somehow been protected from the alienating tactics being used against all three of them, fighting to save my marriage, fighting for our business, fighting to find someone—anyone—to help them and me. Someone who would rescue them from what was happening. That would know what this was and know what to do. Someone who could wake me up from this horrid nightmare and make everything right in my world again, who could just put it all back to the way it was before.

Traumas often come as one specific moment or one incident that changes the trajectory of our lives forever. Traumatic moments desecrate our stories of what should have been and bring us into what we never asked for. And sometimes, the impact of the traumas we experience is continual. In continual trauma, we have events that keep ripping out pieces of our being, making us unrecognizable, like in my story.

But no matter the length of time the attacks come, in one day or over many years, we have choices. We get to choose to live, learn to heal, and learn to rest in our best life, in and through the trauma we are experiencing—or not.

I am still in the middle of my trauma story. I will continue to hold on to hope for the promises of God for restoration. But in the meantime, I'm learning that just because life doesn't look exactly the way I had hoped it would, that doesn't mean my life has to end. God has revealed to me in the many years since then that there's so much to enjoy in this amazing world He has blessed us with, and I cannot stay stuck, curled in a ball on the floor, waiting for what cannot be.

Friend, please turn the page and come with me!

Chapter One

The Plan—Not

My eyes well up, and tears stream down my lightly blushed cheeks. I say a little prayer of thanks for the Holy Spirit's reminder just a few hours before to apply a coat of water-proofer to my mascara. Thank you, Jesus! There will definitely be makeup touchups throughout the day, but at least I won't have black chunks of lash fibers scattered all over my face. I sure wish I had a "proofer" for the swollen eyes that would surely come from a day packed full of joyful tears that I already know will accompany this perfect and momentous day. The tears . . . well, God made me that way! Happy. Sad. Mad. Scared and all the other emotions in between. They bring the tears. That's this girl!

I sit in a comfortably tufted velvet chair in the middle of the gorgeous bridal suite. Tones of soft white, gentle blush, and muted gold surround us in every perfect detail. The spacious bridal suite abounds with tall, elegant windows that let in soft natural light, perfect for capturing the memorable moments and elegant details of my absolutely gorgeous daughter on her wedding day. The subtly sweet smell of fresh flowers and soft, romantic music fills the air, adding to the peaceful and intimate mood encompassing the suite.

She's so happy and full of love for her soon-to-be husband. They're such a beautiful couple, and I beam with the pride of a mama who has imagined what this day would be like for her little girl's entire life. She is my only daughter, and she's as wonderful and as perfect as they come. The hope and excitement of her life with her guy flow from her, and I am grateful to be her mom and blessed to be a part of every wonderfully thought-out detail of this day.

I watch as she sits on a comfortable stool, dressed in her beautiful white silk dressing gown, as curls are crafted in her long blonde hair—the gorgeous hair that most girls would pay big money to have, with its perfect, God-given high and low lights expertly woven throughout her hair. They are the blonde locks that dreams are made of, loosely curled and gently tied back to reveal her beautiful face. The perfection of her makeup makes her look even more angelic than she already is. And I can't help but smile to myself as I silently talk to God and thank Him for this beautiful baby girl that He entrusted me to raise. This special girl made me a mom. It seems like just a few minutes ago. But I've held, raised, and loved her for years. I can't believe I am her mama!

Heart moments flow through my mind. It seems like the years that have passed have gone so quickly as the memories move through my mind at this moment. I see the outline of her tiny feet with tinier toes sticking out from under the skin of my taught belly as she stretches out in her tight quarters. Then I'm holding her for the first time. Her precious face looks at me, and she snuggles in closer. Next came her first steps and her first day of school. I see her holding hands with her best friend as they walk to class together, with her braided hair and backpack, ready for the adventures that lie ahead. My mind replays dance recitals, the first time she pitched in a softball game, her first swim meet, the first boy she liked, and passing her driver's test. I remember homecomings and proms and graduations. My mind recalls her giddy phone calls to tell me

THE PLAN—NOT

about another boy, the one who would soon be her husband, and all of her hopes and dreams of this day and their life together.

She's nervous, I can tell, but I can hear the excitement in her voice as she talks about how much she loves him.

The months leading up to this precious day have been so magical, and I have treasured every moment, including watching her pick out her stunning dress, which makes her look every bit like the princess she is. The perfect flowers and the most delicious cake to be enjoyed by all in attendance sit off to the side. They planned the day together—every detail exactly how they wanted it. All done together to enjoy each other.

She smiles to herself in the sizable vintage vanity mirror, gently pressing her lips together as she glances at the reflection of us both. Her smile changes as her eyes meet mine. She beams at me with the biggest, happiest, most perfect smile there ever was, and she lifts herself out of her vanity chair, walks across the room to where I stand, wraps her arms around me, and holds me tightly. And, as you can imagine, my tears are getting ugly now, so I'm certainly going to need my makeup bag for a touch-up—maybe a re-do.

As I hold this beautiful baby girl of mine, who is all grown, on this day when she is the most beautiful bride there ever was, my body quakes. Oh, my gosh!!! Please, God, keep me steady.

As I have done thousands of times, I whisper to her, "I love you, little girl."

And she responds as she always does. "I love you, little mommy." She takes a deep, steady breath, and I feel the warmth of her peaceful exhale on my neck. Calm and steady. Her embrace is tight, and I feel her love wrapped around me. "Don't make me cry," she whispers, and we both laugh out loud. "Thank you for being here with me, Mom. I wouldn't want to do this without you."

My phone rings, and I know who it is. I've been waiting, somewhat nervously but with so much excitement, all morning for this call. "I promise I'll call you as soon as I'm done!" he had promised me, and I know I'll be his first call. I have not had one minute of productivity today. I just pace and scroll and waste time as one does when one's mind can't focus on anything outside of the call they're expecting at any moment. Any moment now . . .

I answer. "Hey, babe, how's it going?" I ask nervously and hold my breath. My heart is full of hope for him, his dreams, and his future.

"Mom!!! Mom, I did it!!! I passed!! Oh, my gosh! I did it!" And girl, wouldn't you know it; the tears just poured out of me. I gushed alligator tears of pride and love for this sweet boy, who is all grown up and has just made his life dream come true! All the hours, all the money, and all the determination and hard work are wrapped up in this moment.

Since he was a little boy, he always dreamed of becoming a pilot and flying an airplane. Soaring the blue skies and breaking through the clouds. I'm sure the speed of flying was the real passion. The faster, the better. When he was little, his bedroom was adorned with metal airplanes of red and blue that we hung with clear fishing lines from his ceiling so they could fly and soar above him with invisible ease. He even had airplane paintings and pillows. His heart was set.

THE PLAN—NOT

He has worked so hard and now has earned this incredible reward, and I couldn't be prouder of the man he is becoming. He is following his dreams and making them come true.

"I have interviews next week! I did it, Mom!" he tells me with so much excitement pouring out of him. "I'm stopping by. I want to tell Triple, so don't tell him, OK?!" And I promise not to say a word.

When this beautiful boy was born, he was born with an energy like no other! Grandpa called him a tornado, and if you ever get to meet him, he's one you'll never forget. I knew he would do amazing things, but one thing I still know for certain: he is here for a time such as this. He is strong-willed and determined. He has always had a fight in him and a drive to him. He has the biggest heart, and I know he will use this accomplishment to help and love on so many people.

As I wait for him to stop by to share his fantastic news with Dylan, with my lips sealed, I sit in my office on the rug, my back resting on my reading chair, and flip through his old scrapbooks. I look at the photos of this precious boy through the years and remember his youthful laugh. Oh, he has always had one of those contagious laughs, and once he gets started, there's no way you're not laughing with him. He can talk to anyone, anywhere, and when he was young, that was the focus of many parent-teacher conferences. A mama can't get mad if he gets it from her. Am I right?!

If there was someone who needed a friend, this boy was the right guy for the job. I remember his first cross-country meet and his baseball games that were more about talking and making new friends than actually playing the sports. He is an amazing runner and swimmer. He loves tinkering with electronics and gadgets and was the king of Legos back in his day.

The front door opens, and I set down the books resting on my lap and run to him. I wrap my arms around his neck, and he picks me up and squeezes me tight as happy mama tears flow. "I am so very proud of you!!!" I loudly whisper into his neck with what little air I have left in my lungs. He squeezes me tight.

"Thank you, Mom! I love you so much. I couldn't have done it without you."

And here comes Dylan. "What the heck is going on out here?" he asks, and the boy sets me down and lifts his shoulders and chin proudly. As boys do, he puffs up his chest and announces that he did it! This boy, with his heart set, made his dream come true, and Dylan knows just what the boy is talking about. The puffery drops, and they embrace in the biggest hug I've seen them share. My heart is so full, and I beam with love for these two men embracing before me. It's a hug born from many years of deep friendship, a lifetime of encouragement and love. Dylan is a stepfather, a bonus dad, who chose to love these three children, no questions asked, as his own.

When this boy was little, these two were inseparable; you can see this in this perfect moment. The bond they share is unbreakable. And in exceptional dude-like fashion, the embrace ends. They share a moment that leaves me laughing and shaking my head as I wipe the tears from my cheeks. The squishy is over, and the testosterone is back. I am so grateful to be a part of this, so grateful to be Mom to this incredible man!

THE PLAN—NOT

I sit on the deck at the cabin with the cool air on my skin, thinking it's almost time for me to put on a hoodie. My legs are tucked up underneath me in my typical fashion, and I'm listening to two of the kids and their spouses banter back and forth with each other. A wide smile emerges as I wait for the next thing they say or do that will make me shake my head and laugh, and cause my cheeks to hurt. My cheeks always hurt when they're around. They're so funny and bring so much joy to my heart.

The grandkids run around and play all the games they usually play. I love hearing their voices calling to one another and the sounds of their laughter. The fun of kids being kids is my favorite.

Dylan brings me my phone and tells me the other boy is on the line. He and his family are not far away and asking if I need them to stop. "Hey, babe!"

"Hi, Mama! Need anything from the store before we head up the mountain?" He is the one always thinking ahead and making sure everyone is taken care of. The youngest of three, as independent as they come, and strong with a smile that lights up every room. I'm certain that's what stole his wife's heart when they met. It sure steals mine every time I see him!

"We've got it, but you better hurry up. The cousins are ready for their "uncle jungle gym," and they're getting unruly! And this gramma needs some more grand snuggles! Bring me those babies!" I tease.

I slip on my trusty Birkenstocks and wander down the steps to where the grandkids are playing and running. One of my grandsons gently pushes his little sister on the wooden tree swing that Dylan hung just for them. This sweet grandson is so handsome (I had to sneak that in). But for real! They're all the cutest! This little one is cautious to ensure he's not swinging his little sister so high to make her afraid. She smiles, throws her head back, and lets out a huge belly laugh. Her blonde curls flow in the breeze of the forward and back movement of the swing. She's hanging on tightly and loving the attention from her big brother.

There's a gentle breeze, and the smell of pine and bark is just a little stronger than normal. I can hear the birds singing their special songs that I'm sure they've created for just this moment. Pure magic fills the air.

I stand watching and soaking in all that's going on around me. I am the most blessed person I think. I pray silently, thanking God for all that I have. For blessing me so abundantly. For giving me three amazing, beautiful, and healthy children to raise and love and pour into. I express my gratitude because they're all doing well, are grown and married, seem happy, and are living out their dreams and desires. And I have a yard full of grandbabies whom I adore. I can't imagine life being more perfect than it is.

All I ever wanted to be was a mom. And as the kids got older, I couldn't wait for the days of being a grandma. I looked forward to this day and these moments with adoration and longing. I'm here to tell you that it was worth the wait. God has a way of blessing me, and I'm so grateful for all these gifts He has always planned for me.

I love spending as much time as possible with the grandkids. All curled up on the couch, snuggled in cozy blankets, and squished into plenty of pillows, reading books together. I saved favorites from when my kids were small, and the grands love hearing stories their mama and daddy used to read with me. I love kissing the

THE PLAN—NOT

crooks of their necks or the bottoms of their feet (when they were babies) and making them giggle. I love rocking them while they sleep and coloring in coloring books that I picked out special for each one of them. I love taking them on adventure walks around the cabin and teaching them new things, collecting supplies for our next craft gathering and baking session. I love baking with them. And splashing and playing and watching them laugh and swim in the pool. I love Christmas and birthdays and sleepovers and spoiling them as only a grandma can do. I love it all.

"My turn!!! Gramma will push me!" I hear a little one call me out of my gratitude trance, and I, of course, can't resist. "Higher, OK?" he pleads. And my heart is so very happy. So full of joy to have all of this love around me.

This calm only lasts for a few minutes because the later-arriving uncle and his family are pulling into the driveway, and all the kids run to greet them with laughter and stories of the adventures they've had already. An urgency for the rest of the cousins to come and play abounds.

Smiling and patiently waiting my turn, I finally say, "I love you, son! I'm so happy you're all here." I wrap my arms around his waist and squeeze him as I offer another silent prayer, thanking God that He kept him and his family safe. "D's started the grill. I bet you're ready to rest after your shift. Here, let me help you with the baby!" Friend, is there any other way? Of course, I'm taking the baby!

The sun has set, and Dylan and the boys have all pitched in to make the most magnificent fire. The grandbabies are eager to get started on s'mores. The older grandkids know right where I keep the marshmallow roasting sticks and have already brought me the ingredients to prepare little stacks of Grahams and chocolate for them, as I do. They excitedly roast the best-toasted marshmallows ever. Of course, there's competition—there always is! Excited chatter floats all around. And with each moment, my heart swells just like those hot coal marshmallows puffing up over the flames.

I relish the conversation and laughter around the fire. This is one of my favorite parts. I love listening to the kids telling jokes and stories and teasing one another. The big ones engage, and the small ones do too. Having my children and grandchildren all together has been my life's dream. A beautiful, perfect dream.

Our youngest boy sneaks over after coming back from the kitchen. He leans down to my ear and whispers, "I love you, Mama! Thank you for all of this." And then he places a gentle kiss on my cheek. My eyes well up, and I reach to wrap my arms around this grown man and pull him close. This boy is locked in tight when he sets his heart to something. His determination and drive have always been unmatched. This boy made sure we were on a soccer field almost every weekend while he grew up. He has the best heart and has always been there for me and all who are blessed to know him. This boy was always there with a hug and an "I love you" every time they were needed. I could talk to him for hours, and he could hold conversations with any adult at any time. I actually think he may have preferred those conversations. He is unafraid to walk up to anyone and strike up dialogue. He is trustworthy and honest. He is an angel, sent at the most perfect time. He is funny and always brings the fun! And he's loyal. He's a peacemaker, problem solver, and critical thinker. Just all-around joy. When you think about him, *love* is the only word that captures it all. Pure love.

When he was little, I would tell him I loved him, and he would respond, "I love you more!" and I'd say, "I love you most!" and he would always finish the debate with, "I loved you first" and remind me that he picked me to be his mama. I'm not sure how that actually goes down, but I have a good feeling God will have his back on that. He and God are tight.

My heart is full. I am the most blessed and luckiest mama and gramma. I couldn't have imagined a more perfect life. And I have an amazing husband to share it all with. Girl!! I have one of the good ones! He chose to love me and these three children who had a first dad in someone else. He still chooses to pour into them with everything in him—and always has. And I mean everything! When the subject of his falling in love with a woman with three children comes up, he teases and says, "I just added water!" And here we all are! Tada! Just like that. But God knew. God knew that we needed him just as much as he needed all of us.

To blend as we have and be surrounded by all the love that we hold for each other has been the best gift. Life is hard, but it's a little easier when you're surrounded by the people you love the most. That makes all the trials, all the darkness of this world, all of everything that we wouldn't ask for—haven't asked for, that we wouldn't take on if we didn't have to—somehow tolerable. The love of family and having all of your children and grandchildren surround you makes it all manageable. The laughing and the crying. The hard and the good. We do it all together.

But that's not the real story.

Beautiful friend, I wish we were sitting down with our favorite warm beverages in hand, on my comfy couch that boasts too many throw pillows, and with an ultra-soft blanket tucked around our feet. I'd love to share all our beautiful, blessed stories just like these. With many happy chapter endings. To laugh and reminisce, with pure love and joy beaming from our bright smiles and our youthful and rested eyes. I wish we could share in the magic of met expectations and having our perfect dreams fulfilled.

Hoped-for future stories are ones we have told ourselves for our entire lives. They are the stories of what we thought our lives would (should) look like. What we dreamed everything would become. They are the Hallmark movie scripts we "most definitely deserve"—where everything is perfect, and there's always a happy ending to enjoy in just a couple of hours. Hoped-for future stories depict a narrative in which everything unfolds according to plan, and the hard things only last a short while. Even the hardest moments are woven with funny scenes and witty lines, making everything feel a bit lighter.

But we both know we are sitting down with stories very different from these.

As we huddle together with our vastly different stories, the reality of what our experience really is, with the hurts, the darkness, and the frustrations of life just not turning out as we thought they would, weighs us down. Reality calls for us to sit upright at the kitchen table with a fresh box of soft tissues to soak up the tears and the runny sorrow dripping from our noses. We might need a glass of cold water in hand to rehydrate after the tears we shed as we share stories that have left us either grasping at the world for answers or grasping in the direction of the One who created everything, praying for His comfort.

THE PLAN—NOT

Truly hard stories exist, and they produce hearts so broken that we know God is the only way through. These stories bring the kind of pain that invites God to journey with us. To help us heal. To help us survive. To help us forgive. To help us mourn the loss of not only those we love but also mourn the parts of ourselves now missing and the loss of those unmet expectations. No, our stories didn't turn out the way we wanted them to. Some crucial pages were aggressively torn from our book of life, leaving gaps where beautiful memories should have been written.

Because of this, we must invite Him in because we can't do this on our own.

As we journey together through the current chapter of our unmet desires, we must navigate our pain and suffering, which we didn't ask for. Nor deserve. We shoulder this complete brokenness that is so utterly unfair. This story. My story. Your story. The chapters aren't all good, are they?

Here's some truth: even though it doesn't seem like it right now, they're not stories of pain. Even though we've felt and endured more suffering than we ever imagined we could, these are stories of hope. These can be stories of learning about who we are—learning to see ourselves as God sees us. Stories of healing, where we might learn from judgment and persecution. Or learning from the lies the enemy uses to paralyze us and keep us down. Learning about fear. Rejection and betrayal too.

The enemy has stifled us long enough. None of these chapters define who we are. They are not our entire stories. What if it's time that we tell Satan to get out of here and go back to Hell, where he belongs? Tell him that he doesn't belong here anymore.

"Get behind me, Satan! You are a stumbling block to me," says Jesus in Matthew 16:23.

It is time for us to shout it out! We can do so with the mighty power of Jesus because He lives within us (John 14:16-17) — that's the gift He left behind for us when He left this broken garden, His Spirit.

> "GET BEHIND ME, SATAN! You're a stumbling block to me. You've stolen enough from me. I refuse to let you take any more. I have had enough. I refuse to stay stuck in this place for a minute longer. I refuse to live a life of suffering. I deserve to thrive. I belong to Jesus!!!"

Satan only comes to steal, kill and destroy (John 10:10). Period. He prowls around like a roaring lion looking to devour anyone in his path, and apparently friend, we have been in his path.

It is time for us to stand up against him.

It is my prayer that *if* you're feeling less hope than you want, if you're not feeling the comfort, peace, and love you deserve to feel, then as we spend this time together, you might learn to experience *hope*. It's the hope found in the promises and love of a Father who desperately wants us to know Him and to feel His presence — to receive and know this profound and eternal hope. To know who He says we are. And to lean into Him, the One who loves us unconditionally. Only He is big enough to hold our heavy load for us.

Friend, I won't pretend to know everything. I'm just led to share with you some of the lessons I've learned along the way. I'm still in my messy middle, and I'm still learning and healing. And I still get knocked off balance. I don't know the trauma you've endured. I don't know if you are suffering from the loss of someone because

THE PLAN—NOT

of death or putting up boundaries to protect yourself or if you're enduring the same kind of loss as me: parental alienation. Maybe you're healing from an emotional or physical trauma. Or perhaps you're processing pains from childhood. Regardless, please know you are seen and loved. I'm so, so sorry, friend, that you're going through this. There is hope to be found. You deserve to thrive! And I can't wait to share my heart with you.

Come on, let's do this together!

Chapter Two

From Dust to Dust

I have an enormous bedroom. The kind the kids and dog love to run around in because there's ample space. It's pretty funny, actually! When we first moved in, the boys ran and played so hard that we had to repair a hole in the wall within the first few days. This room became our come-together room. Of course, we hung out in the kitchen and family rooms, too, but my bedroom, for some reason, was our laughing and talking and connecting space. We'd sit or lie on the plush carpet and just be together. There were plenty of pillows to cozy up with. Sometimes, one or all the kids would climb onto our bed and participate in the conversation from there. Lying on their bellies, propped up on their elbows, their feet in the air, leaning over the beautiful solid dark wood footboard, they'd blow raspberries on Dylan's cheeks, and the boys would laugh until they cried. This was a place for family meetings and private individual talks, our annual Halloween candy toss, and telling jokes and stories about our days. It was a place for playing and a place for calm, quiet moments. I loved this space and the beautiful memories that were made there, every dream dreamt up and shared there. Even each hug and shed tear.

But one particularly cold winter day brought nothing like the other days. On this day, I lay all alone, right in the middle of the expansive floor, balled up and sobbing uncontrollably. Earlier that day, my world had fallen apart, and I had no idea why or that it was about to get much, much worse. This cry—well, I've never cried this cry before—I had no experience with this kind of absolute horror. I was sobbing so hard that I thought I might throw up. The muscles in my neck and shoulders burned like scorching fire and became hard like concrete. My head throbbed. I didn't know tears had sizes, but as I was about to learn in the many years in front of me, tears most definitely come in sizes. There was no way I could stop what was happening to my body or my life. I felt so very out of control.

With Boy 1's note and then my daughter's attempted note, my entire world fell from around me, and I sank into this horrible pit of a nightmare. One I never asked for. One I never gave my consent to experience. One I could never have imagined would be my reality. How could this happen to us? Would my children come home? When? I wondered what would happen tomorrow or the next day. None of it felt real. This had to be a horrid nightmare, and if I could just wake myself up, it would all be okay.

"Okay" meant my children were home safe, living their best lives, surrounded by our love. It meant I could walk into either of their bedrooms and see them there, sleeping or playing or studying. "Okay" meant his red quilt would be warm with his presence and her possessions would be in constant motion because she was using them.

But they weren't there. His red quilt was cold to the touch and her things were frozen in time. It was not okay!

I don't know what you fear, but my worst nightmare has always been to lose my children. To be forced to do life without them. To never again hear their laughter or watch their smiles light up every room they're in. To not be able to hold them in my arms or tell them how much I love them. To not be able to watch them grow taller and grow up. To not watch baseball games, get them ready for dances, or talk about who they liked in their classes. To not hear how their day went. To not coach them through the hard moments. To not celebrate their wins. Or to not be a part of career decisions and starting a family. My children, from the moment of conception, were my whole world. I lived and breathed for them. When I was going through my divorce, as devastating as that was, I remember saying to myself on many occasions, "At least I'll always have my kids."

My kids are still my everything. All I ever wanted to be was a mom. This was the reason for getting married, though, I admit, I was way too young and naive. But raising children as soon as possible was why I had children at such a young age. I couldn't wait to devote every minute of every day to caring for them, loving them, teaching them, and doing good by them. I tried to, much of the time all on my own.

So, to go through having children, whom I adore beyond any other earthly possession, then losing them and being completely in the dark about what was happening was devastating. And, at that moment, the word *devastating* didn't seem to bring justice to the earth-shattering, total dust-breaking I was going through. I felt isolated. I couldn't speak to them or see them. I didn't know if they were okay. And now, by "okay," I simply meant "safe" and "loved beyond measure." My whole being was torn to shreds in the unknowing.

I couldn't breathe; I couldn't stop the sobbing and I couldn't release the pain. I didn't know what to do. The moments turned into days, days turned into weeks, and weeks turned into months.

On one particularly rough day in the middle of the battle, I knelt in my closet with the door closed behind me. Tears poured down my face, soaking my shirt and my pants. Dozens of fully wet tissues surrounded me, scattered across the floor. My face had fallen to the ground.

After a time, I turned my face upward toward my only comfort. My only hope: Jesus. The bright light inside my prayer closet shone brightly on me as if God Himself was comforting me.

With the door closed, I knew I could be completely raw. I could be the shattered soul I was. I could be naked and real in front of the only One who knew what was happening—and why. The only One who knew what the future held for me and my children.

But on the other side of that door, I had to pretend to be who I was before—the mother I was before my world fell apart.

As time ticked on and help did not come in the way of my kids returning, I grew more desperate. Nobody was saving me or my babies. Police reports, motions with the court, and attorneys with failed promises infiltrated my days. Reunification was not happening. Restoration was not coming. I searched through the internet, trying to figure out what to do, what my options were, trying to understand what process or law was keeping my children from me. The courts were no help. There were no easy legal definitions, no support groups, no information. I couldn't find anything that described what I was going through. I only knew we were under Satan's attack; that was it. I felt so alone. Still, I trusted God could and would say a word to make it all go away.

But He didn't. Not then.

In recent years, I've felt revealed to me that I hadn't discovered parental alienation support groups or connected with other parents who had been alienated from their children, where I could have learned that I wasn't the only one enduring this terrible tragedy, because God was calling me to Him. I believe He was using this inability to find support from other people to draw me closer to Him. So he could comfort me and bring me His eternal hope and His deep peace. He wanted me to depend on Him—as protector *and* sustainer.

> All I had was God.
> All I had were Jesus and the Holy Spirit.

All I had was God. All I had were Jesus and the Holy Spirit. As I felt the gentle nudge of the Holy Spirit call me into my prayer closet to be in the presence of God, time after time, I poured out my heart. I felt His comfort. His strength. His love. I sought Him fully and relied solely on Him. Not others. Certainly not the world or the worldly systems in place. I didn't rely on the comfort of information, support groups, or therapists. Because in the early weeks and months, I couldn't find them. That turned into a blessing. I only sought the comfort God could provide. It was all Him.

A Steady Hand

During this time, I was surrounded by an amazing husband and a son, both of whom, honestly, I don't think I could have survived without. I know my Father in Heaven carried me every moment, but I also know Dylan and my youngest son, through their unconditional love, helped me fight the fight, so to speak. And, as I type this, I hear the Spirit whisper, "But God."

Let's hold here for just a few seconds and feel that together. *But God.*

I was also blessed with dear friends and a precious family who were and still are an incredible support system for me. The hugs, time, and love they poured out over me were an immeasurable blessing. I realized I wasn't all alone. And I am so grateful! I also recognized that they were hurting too. They were enduring loss as well: the loss of my daughter and oldest son — and me, in a sense.

To be honest, though, as large as the role they all played in these painful times, none of them could be my savior. They were not responsible for making any of my crises better or putting life back together for me. I love them — more than they'll probably ever know — and I know God brought them to me on purpose, so I am forever grateful! But Jesus is our Savior, our saving Grace.

This reliance on God didn't make the bad simply go away. My countless hours with Him tucked safely inside the walls of my prayer closet didn't bring my babies back. It didn't allow me to hold them and tell them how much I love them or how sorry I was that this was happening. It didn't set them at the kitchen table after school, so I could hear their beautiful voices and laughter as they told me about their days. It didn't let me be a part of proms, or graduations, or their wedding days.

Rather, my time with God brought me a comfort I didn't have when I sat in front of my computer screen, desperately trying to figure out what this *Twilight Zone* of terror was; I didn't receive this comfort from sitting across a desk with my attorneys, begging them to help me. And I didn't get God's comfort by handing over my credit card to pay for someone with their hand out in the hope that they cared about me, knew how to help, and were equipped to do something to help.

In my prayer closet, I begged and pleaded with God to take the pain away. To bring my kids home. "Please, go get them. Remember, you promised to leave the ninety-nine to go get the one (from Matthew 18:12). And, sir, I'm missing two! A daughter and a son! I can't do this anymore. I can't take it. The pain is too much to endure. Please, help me. I can't breathe; I can't breathe without my children. Please, don't make me do this."

But God

Many months of begging and pleading with God ensued. "What do you want me to do? What did I do? How was I so horrible in my life to deserve this punishment? How can I fix this? How can I make this right? What haven't I repented of? Please, God, just tell me. I'll do anything. Just tell me, and I'll do it now. Please! You gave these precious children to me. You sent them to me to be their mom. You picked me. To love them and take care of them. Why is this happening? Please, let me have my babies back. Please!!!"

Silence.

The painful, gut-wrenching, breath-stealing, heart-shattering agony turned from days of suffering into months, then into years.

Still, silence.

Friend, I imagine you know this kind of loss too. The torment of grief. The torture of unmet expectations and the perceived silence that follows. Perhaps you also know what it's like being broken beyond what you ever thought you could endure. Maybe you've faced your worst nightmare—or are facing it now. Maybe you have relied on our heavenly Father, who loves you more than you could ever imagine, even in the silence. I hope so. He who knows and feels your pain. Every single moment of it. I'm convinced

He would take it all away if that's how our story *was supposed to go*. Maybe you're like me and still in the middle of things. Still learning how to breathe through the mess. Still trying to smile and laugh despite the heartache. And still trying to figure out who this person is that kinda still looks like you but seems so much like a stranger now. The person you could never have imagined you'd become. Do you recognize the face staring back at you in the mirror? The one now learning how to heal? Learning to live. Learning to love again. Learning to do life without large pieces that used to be there.

I wasn't with you in your horrible, life-shattering moments. I wasn't with you while you lay soaking your pillow with alligator-sized tears. I wasn't with you in the moments when you felt alone and afraid. But, friend, I'm with you right now. I am sitting across from you, staring into your pain with so much love for you. With a heart that knows the sorrow you feel and the confidence in a God who has got us.

We are going to do this. We are going to be courageous and heal and stand in hope. We are going to do it together. We are going to get right, right where we are. Because God did not bring us this far to *not* use this pain and suffering and torment for something truly amazing. When God created the earth, He was not done until He said, "It was very good" (Genesis 1:31). And, at this moment, in our brokenness, in our pain, and in our suffering, it is *not* good. Therefore, I know our stories do not end here. We do not end here. This brokenness is not it. It is not over until He can say, "It is very good" for us too! And He will! I just know it!

But first . . . oh boy! Did you know that there was a *but?* God likes buts! And dare I say, He has some big ones! In stories throughout all of Scripture, from Moses to Job and King David to Joseph, and especially with Jesus, God uses *but* to show His grace and intervention. He uses *but* to bring good to our story when we can't see a way through, like with Moses. He reminds us with His *but* that our circumstances are not our defeat, like with Joseph. He uses *but* to remind us that ashes aren't the end of our stories. Isn't all of that exactly what we are in need of in this place? When all seems lost, He introduces a *but*. We can insert our own big giant God-but right here.

I was crushed to dust, but . . .

Ooooh! Are you starting to like His *but* also? Funny—the world will tell us that *but* is a negative word and that everything before the *but* is a lie. But, [winking!] with God, everything is better on the other side of the *but*. And there's certainly truth before it. We can attest to that.

Yes, horrible things happened. But . . .

Yes, there is pain and suffering. But . . .

Yes, you're hearing lies and feeling neglected. But . . .

Yes, things aren't the way we want. But . . .

Yes, there is fear. But . . .

Yes, there are persecutions and attacks. But . . .

Yes, this freaking sucks. But . . .

Yes, we're spending more time in the hard moments than we thought we could endure. But . . .

God didn't just redeem us for Himself; He will redeem our stories for Himself as well. We are already His—and so are our stories. All of them, including the ones filled with pain and suffering. And He will use all of this for His glory. The win is His forever!

> "But as for you, ye thought evil against me: But God meant it unto good" (Genesis 50:20, KJV).

I don't know about you, but this actually gets me excited. So does this:

> "My flesh and my heart faileth: but God is the strength of my heart, and my portion for ever" (Psalm 73:26, KJV).

The past several years have helped me know this to be true.

But God . . .

I hold on to these two words. God will make this good, and He is the strength of my heart forever! Breathe this in, friend.

Made New in the Potter's Hands

Down the road from the crisis, you may remember the anguish or have a moment—because no matter how long it's been since we went through the thing that ground us to complete dust, we will still have moments when the tears flow, times when the heart hurts again. When we can't seem to motivate ourselves to stop scrolling on our phones or wash our hair. Often, they come during birthdays, anniversaries, or holidays like Christmas. You might be walking through a department store, passing by the baby section, when suddenly, tears stream down your cheeks as you become overwhelmed by the intense love you long to share with the ones you've lost. Strangers' faces will communicate curiosity about our sudden outbursts. The old CD case or the record sitting on the shelf might flood us with memories of the music from that time. These moments, and many other triggers, might cause liquid sorrow to well up in our eyes. Thankfully, we can take a beat and smile through the tears, lifting our eyes to our Father, who loves us abundantly, and proclaim, "But God!"

We need to trust Him in and through our stories and allow Him to mold our dust into a new kind of beautiful masterpiece. A new kind of whole. A new creation. *But God!*

When God created the world, He formed us from dust. Genesis 2:7 says, "Then the LORD God formed man from the dust of the ground and breathed into his nostrils the breath of life, and the man became a living being."

Friend, God created us from dust, and this proves that, in our complete brokenness, when we feel we've become dust again, nothing is too big of a job for Him to reconcile. He will mold us, heal us, and breathe the breath of life into us once again—if we allow Him. "Cannot I do with you as this potter? saith the LORD. Behold, as the clay is in the potter's hand, so are ye in mine hand" (Jeremiah 18:6, KJV).

> He is holding all of us in His hands. Every grain of dust that formed us, He knows as He holds them in His hands.

What a promise! He is holding all of us in His hands. Every grain of dust that formed us, He knows as He holds them in His hands.

Did you know that pottery symbolizes renewal? It's a reflection of starting again and being reborn. When we are broken beyond recognition, God can use all of our broken pieces and all of our dust to make us new, to make us something beautiful. We can be reborn into something necessary and important. In this learning how to do life after the brokenness, we still get to be whole and beautiful and loved. Because we are loved! Oh, so loved!

We are given the opportunity, right here and right now, to allow Him who loves us more than any other, to be our potter once again, molding us into the person He created us to be. We can't change what's happened to us, what's brought us so much pain—we can't change what's taken the life right out of our souls and the breath right out of our lungs—but, beautiful friend, we *can* allow Him to make us into something new and whole and so, so beautiful once again. But God!

Surrendering to God's Plan

In Genesis 22, we read the story of Abraham and Isaac. God calls Abraham to bring Isaac, his only son, whom God confirms that He knows Abraham loves, to a mountaintop to be given as a burnt offering—to sacrifice him. Did you catch that? God confirmed to

Abraham that He knew and understood that Isaac was his one and only beloved son.

I'm just sitting here, thinking about those two dreadful days when I lost two of my children. I picture God standing before me, saying, "Shawna, I know I gave these miracles to you, and I know you love them more than anything you could have ever imagined . . . they're your whole world. I get that. But there's this thing I want you to do . . ."

Eeeek! Ummm, nope! No way! What?!

Could you do it? Could you receive God's request and agree to this insane plan? Then go wake up your child early, who is all sleepy and snuggly, with eyes looking up at you, full of love and the knowledge that you are a protector as you cradle them in your arms. You're their entire world. They trust you with everything. You've been their provider with unconditional love. You scoop them up, tuck them into the car, and fasten their seatbelt to keep them safe, knowing you've been asked to give them up to something bigger and unknown. That you must give them over and never see them again. That you must trust God. And you must be obedient *and* have faith. Sounds like a horrible movie I'd never watch! Sounds like a devastating story on the news, and after seeing it, you know the person has lost their ever-loving mind. Nope! Not this girl.

God's Word calls us to obedience and faith. If we sat together, I'd tell you that I strive to be both of those things: obedient and faithful. But if I had known I'd have to sacrifice my children — not be able to hug them or be with them or hear them tell me silly jokes or watch them live their lives — and be called to that level of obedience and faith? I don't know if I could have done that on my own. If I'd known ahead of time what I would be asked to do, I think I would have been disobedient and not faithful at all.

You know, we can't have an authentic, stable faith if everything is always easy. We can only have that kind of faith in the uneven parts of our path. God doesn't wait for us to be ready. Or maybe He doesn't wait for us to think we're ready.

We don't get to say, "OK! I'm ready to practice my faith. Give me something hard!" That's just not how it works.

> If I'd known I'd be doing life without my children, I would have never agreed to the plan that lay before me.

If I'd known I'd be doing life without my children, I would have never agreed to the plan that lay before me. Never. I wouldn't have volunteered to live out that kind of commitment. I'm just not strong enough on my own. But here I am. *But God.* He is here too! Always here and always faithful. Always by my side. And in these times of pure devastation and unquenchable pain, He has carried me. I know I could never have made it on my own.

But God.

Bob Marley once said, "You never know how strong you are until being strong is the only choice you have."

Will it be worth it? This non-choice we find ourselves in?

My answer is a shaky yes, but a yes nonetheless. Why? With God, we don't have to do it alone. We are never alone. There is peace in the faith and joy in the obedience. But sometimes . . . I might just need a minute.

Chapter Three

Anchor of Hope

*I*t might be a little early in the book to insert this gem, but here we go anyway. We need to remember that God loves us too much to answer our prayers in any other way than the right way and at any other time than the right time. Friend, do you believe that? Is this where your hope lives?

You know that saying, "Take one day at a time"? During this early time in my trauma journey, I was literally surviving minute by minute, every day. I know sometimes I was only making it through one second at a time. It was in these moments that I couldn't do it on my own. There was no way I could take the credit for making it through the raw part of my journey. God carried me, one hundred percent.

He was there when I couldn't even function. When I couldn't breathe. When I was standing in the shower with hot water flowing over me, sobbing for what seemed like forever. On the days that I didn't remember the drive to work and had driven there on autopilot. Or when someone asked for me at the office and I was hiding under my desk (literally!) because I just didn't have the strength to smile and pretend one more time that day. When I didn't know what the next painful thing was that was coming at me. When the next email that tore me to shreds would come or when people showed up with false allegations or additional horror. I can assure you that I didn't survive all that on my own. It was in those moments that I was carried.

As a child, I loved the poem "Footprints in the Sand," by Mary Stevenson. The words just had a way of speaking to me. I love it even more today. I live out the words. I know there was not a moment of suffering that I walked alone. It was and is God who carries me.

It was in these lonely and dark moments that I learned complete and pure dependence on Him. When I was at my worst, I sought Him. In the pit in which I found myself, where there was nothing in my power I could do, when nothing was available to me to fix the situation, nothing to put it back the way it was, I still had God, the Creator of everything. No attorney, law enforcement agency, or judge could help. Just God. My hands were tied, and I felt as if I was held captive and in a prison of time and procedure — torture — so I leaned in ever closer to my Savior.

I soon had an awakening in that pit. What if He was calling me to this deep place, where I felt lonely, hopeless, and isolated, because He wanted me to rely on Him — and Him alone?!

> My only hope. The source that keeps replenishing itself.

After all, it was there, in the utter darkness, that He called me to Him most loudly. Where He embraced me and taught me how He would never leave me. I learned in the dark to connect to Him as the Light, the source of my hope. My only hope. The source that keeps replenishing itself.

God didn't keep me in this particularly dark season of unknowing forever. Just long enough to rely on Him. His compassion coaxed me to turn to Him with every unstable step I made, and He held me steady. Even though I still couldn't get the help I wanted from the legal system and God didn't deliver me out of despair, I learned what we were going through. I learned a name for what was happening: *parental alienation*. And I learned I wasn't the only parent going through this type of torment. The information I learned didn't fix anything or make it stop. The knowing didn't bring my daughter and son back, but it did help me to know that it wasn't just me or my family suffering. I wasn't losing my mind. There are psychologists and doctors who very much knew what was happening to my children and all that was intertwined with it. Once I learned what this specific pathology was, I read literature and learned more. Knowing didn't bring peace, and it most certainly didn't bring hope.

But God.

Elie Wiesel once said, "Just as man cannot live without dreams, he cannot live without hope. If dreams reflect the past, hope summons the future."

I had a belief that the "system" — the attorneys, the police, and the counselors — would make things right. I believed they would see the wrong and make it right. That they would see what was broken and would help our family. But they didn't. Humans failing me brought me to a place where I learned to stand firmly on the phrase, "I will put my hope in you, Lord."

Hope didn't and still doesn't make what happened to me and my children disappear. It doesn't make it right. Or less hurtful or lonely. It doesn't make the persecution or judgment go away or feel any less painful. *But hope gives us a future, something to live for*. Hope is trusting that God has a plan—a good one—even if we can't see it.

I learned to let Him anchor me in truth and to steady me in the storms that came. They still come. And I'm certain life will never be storm-free, so I'm thankful for this lesson.

Jesus is Our Anchor in the Storm

> "We have this hope as an anchor for the soul, firm and secure" (Hebrews 6:19).

In the first century, Christians were persecuted, even martyred for their faith. They were beaten, tortured, thrown into the dens of ravenous lions, and even burned at the stake. Roman Emperor Nero was a ruthless leader who set out to take down and destroy all of Jesus's followers.

To encourage one another discreetly and stay as safe as possible, these early Christians used a secret symbol to declare unity under Christ's lordship. The symbol was that of an anchor. You can find anchors on countless tombstones located in Rome, Italy, in the St. Domitilla and Priscilla cemeteries.

> We will be battered by the tortuous waves of life, but letting down a steady anchor will ultimately keep us from crashing against the rocks.

The anchor steadies a vessel in turbulent waters. It holds it secure and safe. We will be battered by the tortuous waves of life, but letting down a steady anchor will ultimately keep us from crashing against the rocks..

Today, we still see the anchor displayed as a symbol throughout our culture. People wear it on jewelry, print it on coffee mugs, and tattoo it on their bodies. But beyond the physical representations, we need the anchor engraved on our hearts, for hope is the anchor for our soul, always firm and secure.

Left to its own, our heart is restless. It struggles and thrashes about. It's desperately sick and hurting and needs help (Jeremiah 17:9). Our hearts aimlessly ride the waves of our busy lives and all we endure, but we need to cling to something deeper and stronger than the surface waters. We need to commit to and trust God. We need to anchor our hearts in God and His truths. We must continue to connect to our true source of hope (Romans 15:13). We must anchor ourselves in God.

> "I waited patiently for the LORD to help me, and he turned to me and heard my cry. He lifted me out of the pit of despair, out of the mud and the mire. He set my feet on solid ground and

> steadied me as I walked along. He has given me a new song to sing, a hymn of praise to our God. Many will see what he has done and be amazed. They will put their trust in the LORD"
> (Psalm 40:1-3, NLT).

First, we wait patiently for the Lord to help us. Though it's hard to wait in the pain and suffering, we must anchor ourselves in His truth and wait on Him. He always hears our cries. I have felt Him turn to me and comfort me. After a time, He lifts us up out of all the mud and muck we've been dredging through, and He gently plants us on solid ground, making sure we're steady and stable.

I learned to keep walking. I'll keep moving forward. I hope you do too. That's what this book is about.

Bound by Grace

There's a song that came out during the time I was going through my divorce by Rodney Atkins called "If You're Going Through Hell." Do you know it? It was my theme song during this season in the pit (i.e., Hell), but even then, I didn't know how much worse my story would get. Friend, there are times when the suffering we endure sure feels like Hell. Please don't stop. Don't stay here. We can't let Satan win.

Oh, Satan knows we're there in the pit! But I also know that our Father in Heaven has us. We must hold on to hope for our future. God is with us right now. In these very hard moments. We don't have to wait for something in our situation to change before we can hope. Before we can receive His blessings and promises. We don't have to hope for Him. We just need to receive Him. He is with us right now. Every step of the way. In the pain. In the darkness. In the hope. In the praise.

It is an honor to receive His blessings, but not before we're ready. He knows when we're ready. God must pull us out of the mud before we can stand on His solid ground. Cries will come before praise. Pain turns into promises, and those promises turn into the best praise. "You are my refuge and my shield; I have put my hope in your word." (Psalms 119:114).

> "But those who hope [qavah] in the LORD will renew their strength. They will soar on wings like eagles; they will run and not grow weary, they will walk and not be faint" (Isaiah 40:31).

The Hebrew word *qavah* in this passage means "hope," but a more accurate translation of this word is "To wait with expectancy. To look for." Or "To lie in wait for." Knowing the intention behind this word, we can eagerly look for, expect, and wait on the Lord to renew our strength. This word *hope* isn't a passive hope that someday God's promises will come to us. It is an active hope that says we know His promises are ours for the taking, and we sit in expectancy for the promised blessings to arrive.

Qavah has another definition in the Bible: "To bind and gather." Hope in God is an act of binding His promises to ourselves. We must choose, even in the most painful of times, to bind all of our hurts and trauma with His truths. We must bind these moments with His love. His healing. His provision. Often, we don't have hope because we simply have not chosen hope. We've chosen pain, despair, or victimhood instead. But we can change that right now.

We can choose Him.

From Brokenness to Beloved

God designed our bodies to heal physically (James 5:15). In fact, I've seen His healing firsthand, hundreds, if not thousands, of times. If we recognize the stressor that our body is experiencing and remove it, our bodies can and will heal. God is amazing, and His design is perfect. I am learning to have that same knowledge in His ability to heal all the other aspects of my life. Even though our physical healing may not come as we think it might, God redeems all things. We must bind our reality to His truths. If we can let Him take our emotional pains and stressors, our emotional injuries, we can and will heal in these areas too. Just like with our physical healing.

> *"For I will restore health unto thee, and I will heal thee of thy wounds, saith the LORD"* (Jeremiah 30:17, KJV).

To heal emotionally, we can access God's certainty and hope, as well as the happiness that flows from Him. This is accomplished through knowing the voice of our Father in Heaven, just as John 10:27-28 tells us: "My sheep listen to my voice; I know them, and they follow me. I give them eternal life, and they shall never perish; no one will snatch them out of my hand."

The time is *now* for us to hear His voice. To know His promises. To put our trust in Him, as He pulls us out of this pit. He will plant us on solid ground. And even though we cannot see what the healing and the future may look like right now, we can trust in Him. Friend, let's release the outcome and give it all to Him. Let us hope. Let us make way for Him to renew our strength and not stay stuck. I have no doubt that He's even calling us to soar!

But what if your hope has been manifesting in the wrong place? What if your hope was in thinking it would all be put back in place, like before? And only in that place, can you heal. That was me for a long time. I just wanted Him to put it all back together and tie it up with a big, red bow. Life was great! It felt so good in that place. I was finally happy. So I wanted it all back.

We must remember God knows the future. Maybe what we thought was good was not His best for us. Honest moment here: it's hard to imagine better than it was. Am I right? But what if the old life would have left us far from Him? What if that perfection we felt was false security and would have led us down the wrong path? What about the intimacy we can have with God now? Because of this!

A belief is something that is accepted and considered to be true. A belief can be an opinion and can change. So our beliefs become "our" truths. For instance, I believe that coffee beans are magic beans that bring smiles and joy, and I love starting my day with my magic beans. But, for someone else, coffee beans are not so magical. Maybe even gross! What we believe is based on specific information that we have at any given time. Our beliefs can change in an instant. The problem with believing is when we allow our beliefs to become our realities when they don't match up to who God says we are or what He says is truth. God is not only absolute hope but also absolute truth.

Here is some of His Truth:

- He says we are His (John 1:12).
- He says He loves us, and we are chosen (1 Thessalonians 1:4).
- He says we are holy and beloved (Colossians 3:12).
- He says we are redeemed (Romans 3:24).
- He says the Holy Spirit dwells in us (1 Corinthians 3:16).
- He says we are triumphant (2 Corinthians 2:14).
- He says we are new (2 Corinthians 5:17).
- He says we are set free (Galatians 5:1).
- He says we are blessed in every spiritual blessing (Ephesians 1:3).
- He says we are forgiven by the grace of Christ (Ephesians 1:7).
- He says we were formerly darkness, but now we are light (Ephesians 5:8).

- He says His peace guards our hearts and minds (Philippians 4:7).

God didn't design us with these problems that we have and are going through. These problems, pains, and traumas are not who we are. They're just what we are experiencing. We are His. We are His perfect creation. He loves us. We need to stop holding onto these false truths about ourselves. We do not need to be stuck in this horrible place, wondering if the enemy's words are true. We need to do the healing.

There's a fine line here that separates the brokenness from the healing. If we constantly tell ourselves that we are broken and traumatized by what we've been through, we will receive that as our truth. That will become who we are. We will stay stuck in that. And we can't afford to stay there, in that lie. That's not who we are. We are healed. And whole. And loved. We just have to choose that to be our truth. And we need to keep choosing it over and over again until it becomes not just our belief but our reality. Our absolute truth.

> "We are troubled on every side, yet not distressed; we are perplexed, but not in despair; Persecuted, but not forsaken; cast down, but not destroyed" (2 Corinthians 4:8-9, KJV).

My dear friend, we will have trouble in this world (John 16:33). Sometimes, it will be trouble within us. Other times, trouble finds us. But we are not alone. Troubled is not how our story ends. These old hurts and persecutions cannot be our absolute truth. Our promise is so much greater than this distress and despair! The promise is that we are neither destroyed nor forsaken. We have been set free! We can stand on this firm ground right now. Even if we're still hurting. Even if we're still in the messy middle. Even though we are standing in *The Twilight Zone*, with the world spinning around us, stealing our breath and knocking us off-balance.

But God.

My hope is in you, Lord!

My friend, our dreams of old reflect the past. All that once was need not be again. All that we had expected life to be like is not necessary. Those dreams are in the past. That was the old us, before all of this happened. We are becoming something new. Something better. God is taking us to new places. He is forming us into who He wants us to be, in the future He wants us to have. Our hope, especially our hope in Him, is what summons our future. How about we step into that together? How about we allow God to renew our strength? Let Him take away our weariness and help us soar on His promise like eagles! Let us hope in the Lord and renew our strength. Let us rest in His promises for our future and trust that He loves us so much — that He will make things good.

Chapter Four

I Need a Minute

Years ago, over several summers when the kids were younger, we enjoyed an annual beach vacation for a couple of weeks in Hawaii. These beautiful memories and moments will be forever ranked among my favorites. When they were babies, I always dreamed of someday taking them to the beach and spending entire days in the sunshine with the beautiful powdery white sand clinging to their beautiful brown, sun-kissed skin. I relished watching them run and play and jump into the white-capped waves. I feel so blessed to have that branded into my memories.

I loved taking surfing lessons with the kids and building sandcastles and villages, complete with moats filling up with the incoming tide. I used to bury the kids and Dylan in the sand and listen to their belly laughs born from all the fun. We'd take long walks and get the best shaved ice available. (If you haven't had shaved ice with macadamia nut ice cream on the bottom, you're missing out!) We spent our days together, shopping and eating and playing. We went on hikes and witnessed the picturesque waterfalls and the magic of seeing the entire island from a helicopter for the first time. We stayed in a bamboo jungle house with lizards scaling the beams above us and in an oceanfront condo with a staff that told us stories of famous actors who'd stayed there while filming their hit movies. We enjoyed treats at the coffee shop and local bakeries and tours of so many fun local farms, factories, and towns. But my favorite part was that we could forget the rest of the world and all of its drama and pain and just be together—playing, talking, singing, joking, and making memories together. Oh, the laughing. I miss that most.

During these precious times away with all of them, I loved how I could escape the continuous battle of life—and what I felt deep inside. It seemed like every time I turned around, there was another spiritual or physical attack. Another piercing back kick to my gut. On one of these trips, the stress of life on top of these attacks felt so constant and heavy before leaving that I looked forward to the getaway even more than normal so I could flee from everything and everyone.

On this particular trip, we visited a beach that had much stronger waves than our normal spot, and the kids wanted to play with their body boards. I remember trying to stand in the ocean with the large, unruly waves breaking all around me. They crashed into me and completely knocked me off balance. While throwing me all around, I grew a bit nervous. I had the opportunity to walk out before the next wave rolled up—to get back to the safety of the sand and the stillness of the beach—but before I could escape the next crash of water, I was struck by a large and aggressive wave. It took me under. As I struggled to figure out which way was up and plant my feet firmly on the sandy bottom and get my bearings, I was forced to endure being underwater a bit longer by the tumbling violence. In those additional seconds, as I was thrashed and thrown about, rolled over, and completely out of control, I realized that was exactly what I was feeling in my life. I was feeling thrown around, beaten, and attacked. Pummeled. One thing had been happening right after another. Being thrown about in the ocean seemed to become a visual and experiential picture for me, something to which I could relate.

> Friend, Satan wants to keep us paralyzed and stuck.

Friend, Satan wants to keep us paralyzed and stuck. He wants to keep us defeated and broken and hopeless. He wants us discouraged and alone. He wants us to be afraid. He wants us completely broken. He will send constant roaring waves to knock us off balance over and over and keep our heads underwater, barely able to catch a breath. It's in these moments that he hopes we will give up and give in. It's in these times of trial that he tries to make us weak, hits us hard enough—and constant enough—to make the next blow the one that makes us crumble. His desire is to steal, kill, and destroy so he can come in and take over completely (John 10:10).

When I have been submerged in my hardest moments, I can visualize my face, tipped slightly upward and completely submerged in water. I have the tiniest of straws (picture those itty bitty black stir straws at some coffee shops) pressed tightly between my lips so that water doesn't fill my mouth. The other end of the stir straw reaches just above the waterline. I am breathing. But barely. Just the tiniest amount of air makes it through, enough to survive. Barely. I'm holding on just a little bit longer.

I have had times when I have felt like I'm more drowning than breathing. It's in these moments that I am most grateful for the Holy Spirit and the quiet whisper that leads me right to my prayer closet. The moments when I fall to my exhausted knees and proclaim, "Father, I just need a minute." With my head falling forward, chin to my chest, and the tears no longer held back, as sobs and pain release, I cry out, "I just need a minute!"

That's my way of asking God to let me catch my breath. Not just a smoothie-sized straw breath, but a breath so much bigger — one that fills my lungs and lifts the heaviness from my chest. If He's allowing me to face these crashing waves, there must be a purpose for the storm. He has a why. And I may not understand the why right now, but it's there. God knows. And this is my reminder that I can't do it on my own. When the weight of everything is far too much, when the waves keep getting stronger and stronger and I'm knocked so far off-balance that I don't know which way is up, and when my chest hurts because my lungs can no longer move the air through my wrecked body, the Holy Spirit prompts me to go to my closet and receive the stillness, the love, the joy, the peace, and the gentleness that I so desperately need in that moment — a comfort that nothing on earth can give me. "Thy will, Father. But please, I just need a minute."

Divide and Conquer

> It's not over until God says, "It is good." Remember that. Tuck it into your heart today and carry it with you.

You don't deserve this suffering. You are not stuck. You are not defeated. You are not hopeless. You're not helpless. I'm sure you're feeling these things. I'm sure you're feeling paralyzed and broken. Oh, how I wish I could be there to give you my best big hug and remind you that you are not all of those lies the evil one so convincingly tries to make you believe. My friend, this is not the end. It's not over until God says, "It is good." Remember that. Tuck it into your heart today and carry it with you.

And until that time when He proclaims that it's all good again, we're going to do this hard thing. We are going to heal and learn, and we are going to fight the good fight!

We are called to endure tribulation. We will be called to endure crushing fear and horribly painful judgment. We will be in positions that cause us to endure more than we thought we could bear. And alone, it would be. Remember, Satan wants us paralyzed, but God calls us transformed (2 Corinthians 5:17). Friend, which do you want?

I'm convinced Satan's primary goal is attacking the family. He's been heavily attacking my family since the events that led to my divorce from my first husband. His goal is to rip families to shreds at the seams, tearing husbands and wives apart. He whispers lies into unexpecting ears and turns family members against each other, making them forget the commands to forgive, to love, and to serve. He's taking children of all ages away from their parents through addiction, abduction, and alienation.

You can look around anywhere in the world today and witness all of his devastation on the family. If Satan gets one person away from the family, he attacks them individually while they're alone, whether it's a separation by one room or thousands of miles. Lies, anger, sin, drugs, disrespect, unforgiveness. Everywhere we turn, we can see the weapons and byproducts of his tactics. He's not that creative. They're always the same.

> The enemy will tell you that all of this pain and sorrow and suffering crashing down around you in massive waves of defeat is because of you.

The enemy will tell you that all of this pain and sorrow and suffering crashing down around you in massive waves of defeat is because of you. Your sin. What you've done wrong. And he will use others to tell you that you don't deserve to be happy. You don't deserve to live a joyful life. He will use others to persecute you and judge you. His message is someone like you doesn't deserve the blessings that others get to have. He will turn you against yourself, so eventually, you'll be telling yourself those same lies.

In John 9, we read the story about Jesus and a blind man. This man had been blind from birth. That's a key point here. As Jesus and His disciples passed by the man, the disciples asked Jesus who sinned to make the man blind. Was it him or his parents? I know you know the answer, but I'm going to remind you because, in your hurting, you deserve to be reminded. The answer is neither! Neither the man nor his parents sinned. He did not do anything to warrant being born blind or to suffer persecution or judgment. He didn't deserve this condition. This was not a consequence. The man had struggles so God could create this moment—one in which Jesus could show the miracles and mercies of God! And your tough seasons are times when God can show up and show off His miracles and mercies in your life and through your story also! Don't let the enemy tell you otherwise. Don't listen to his lies!

Shadows of Deceit

Many times, in gut-wrenching sobs on my prayer closet floor, I have begged God to show me what I did to deserve the pain and heartbreak I was living through. I asked Him in moments of complete and utter devastation *why* He was punishing me. I was afraid that I'd done something horribly wrong to deserve the attacks that seemed to come at regular and continuous intervals. And worse, I didn't even know what I'd done that was so horrible that I should be suffering so deeply. What would someone have to do to have their biggest and best blessings taken from them? The gifts that God Himself felt I was worthy to receive and trusted me with to love as He loves—to have those blessings torn from my arms . . .

I'm not saying that we've been perfect our whole lives. I'm not saying that we haven't done anything wrong. Because we are imperfect humans, and we make mistakes, and in our imperfections, we've hurt people. And we must take responsibility for the wrongs we've done. Our repentance for what we've done is between us and our Father in Heaven, and when necessary, asking for forgiveness and paying retribution to those we've hurt is necessary. What I'm talking about here is when Satan tries to keep us downtrodden and full of fear to control us. To keep us hurting and broken and to keep us from being who God designed us to be. To prevent us from doing what God leads us to do. To keep us stuck so the world can't see God's mercies and grace through us. Make sure you receive this right here. Satan wants to keep us stuck right here in this misery so those around us won't see God's mercies and grace.

> *"Satan wants to keep us stuck right here in this misery so those around us won't see God's mercies and grace."*

Satan wants our light to be hidden under a bowl (Luke 11:33), and he will use whatever lies possible to keep us down.

If you didn't do anything to cause the pain you're in—and to be honest, even if you did, rest assured that God is still going to use it—just like He did with the blind man, He will use your pain to show the world His goodness through miracles. Through these hard and painful moments of suffering and enduring, the works of God are manifested. They are displayed in Him. These miracles are His power and the working of Him. And He has many miracles and mercies set aside for you! Even in your harshest seasons of pain. Even when it doesn't seem like there's any way back from it all. They're already there for you. He's waiting for you to receive them!

Awakening to the Goodness of God

Friend, let's have a heart-to-heart. Do you ever doubt the blessings of Jesus? His dying on the cross to forgive your sins? Do you believe in the finished work of the cross? Let's pause here and take a moment to ponder these questions. Because if you doubt these truths, you will doubt God's promises for good things in your life. You will believe you only deserve the bad things. You will fear consequences from God and the punishment of mankind. And you'll believe you deserve the latter.

None of these promises or truths of God's goodness means we won't suffer in this life. Bad things happen. "I have told you these things, so that in me you may have peace. In this world you will have trouble. But take heart! I have overcome the world." (John 16:33). We live in a broken garden. But these promises from God do mean that we are forgiven, and the premise of our story is not to live a life of punishment and pain but to live a godly life fit for our position as inheritors.

Do you have the wrong conclusions about God? Do you think He's a punisher? Do you think you deserve the pain and suffering you've been enduring because you've done something to deserve it? May I remind you the Word of God tells us that those who follow Jesus and live godly lives will suffer persecution (2 Timothy

3:12). Maybe this point is important enough to be read again: *those who follow Jesus and live godly lives will suffer persecution.*

I have sat in desperation, thinking the only acceptable goodness in my crisis would be if God waved His hand and put it all back the way it was. If He just put it all back to the way I wanted and restored the story of how I thought it would go, then I could heal. Then I could be happy. Then I could smile and laugh and enjoy all of my blessings again. Only then, I thought, would He have kept His promise to make all things good (Romans 8:28).

Maybe that's where you are today. If we think the goodness of God comes only in the way we want it to unfold, putting it all back to the way it was before the hurt and brokenness, then we will surely miss out on His true goodness. We just won't see it if we're too busy looking for what we previously had or expect instead of discerning what He is bringing us to in the aftermath.

His goodness doesn't mean everything will go our way, the way we want it to go. We need to trust that He sees the entire picture and knows what's best for us. It's important to release His goodness to Him so He can do His thing.

We can pray together, "I love you, and I trust you. Please show me your goodness in this season." We must be open to hearing from Him and seeing what He has in store for us in all things. That's the hardest part: laying it at His feet and not picking it back up.

The Freedom of Release

Imagine with me for a moment . . . we both have our arms full, loaded with heavy and horribly painful moments, big and bigger and probably some smaller ones too. There are many forms of hurt, heartache, betrayal, shame, sickness, and pain. Our arms are also full of the loved ones we pray for, our shortcomings, the things we are asking God for, and the things we need His forgiveness for. We are also carrying our big hopes and our God-sized dreams.

Still imagining, together, we go visit our Father in Heaven with our arms wide and heavy with our whole hearts and all of our hurts. We come near to Him, and while standing before Him, we say, "Father, all of this load is just way too much for me to carry on my own. I just can't do it anymore. Thank you for offering to take these from me and making my load lighter. Thank you for receiving this burden. Thank you for loving me and making all of this good. I know you love me so much, and I trust you that you know better than I do. I've decided that I'll let you work this all out on my behalf. Here, I leave it all for you."

He smiles and pulls us in and wraps His big daddy arms around us. He hugs us and assures us that we're going to be just fine. He reminds us of how much He loves us and how He will forever be with us. He reminds us we are faithful, and our coming to Him is exactly what He wanted us to do. He rejoices in us for bringing our heavy loads to Him so He can help make our burdens less. We turn to walk away, feeling so much lighter and even more loved and more confident in our journey ahead. We understand we aren't in it alone, and it feels so good to be so supported and free. We, you and I, smile in relief.

But then we stop. Turn on our heels, our shoulders lifted high and our backs straight with pride, and we walk back over to where God is, with all that we set down before Him rests. We look Him right in the eyes, giving Him an unsure kind of look. We bend over and pick up several of the items that we'd left for Him to carry for us. And in this moment, we say, "Sorry. Ummmm, I actually don't trust you with this . . . and maybe this. Oh, and this one too. So I'll just take these back with me. I think I've got a better handle on this than you do. I think I know how to fix this one better now."

Ouch! Let's not do that!

God wants to release us from our burdens. He wants to love us through our hurt. He wants to carry our heavy-laden loads for us. But if we keep picking our junk back up, taking it back, and not trusting Him to do what's best for us, He can't. He won't.

We need to trust Him. And we need to give Him what we don't have control over. We need to do our part. We need to take action—like pray, serve, take care of our bodies, rest—and do the things we can with what God has given us. We need to heal. We need to move forward. We need to forgive. We need to do the work. But when there's nothing left that we can do, we need to lay everything at His feet and let Him have it all. And trust Him. We need to avoid picking up all the pain and suffering again to carry it alone.

Friend, it's okay to take a moment to feel your pain. I believe we have to feel it to move through it. Grieve. Take the time. Pray. Cry. Journal. Seek outside help if you need it. But please don't unpack and stay where you are. Here, in the hurting, is not your home. Here is not where you're supposed to be. You're supposed to be in the folds of God's arms, in the place of healing and joy. Grace and peace. We aren't supposed to carry all the pain and suffering. We just aren't. That's why we're here together. Together, through these pages, we are going to feel and heal. And when God calls out our restoration and pours it out over us, we'll be ready for it!

Embracing His Ever-Present Peace

I enjoy living in Arizona and getting outdoors in God's wondrous beauty during most of the year. Actually, it's all year because even when it's super-hot, we are a short drive to where it's not so bad. I am thankful I can walk out my front door and move my body and be in God's Creation and find solitude. I often walk and hike by myself so I can have time to pray and spend time with Him. I often talk to Him the entire time I'm out. If you happen to be on a trail and hear me talking to myself, rest assured, I'm not crazy! I'm just talking to God.

I consider it a privilege to thank Him for all the beauty that surrounds me. He creates some incredibly amazing things to see, and I love experiencing it all. I thank Him for my healthy body, which allows me to be active, out witnessing so many magnificent sights. I love to hear the birds chirping and singing as I pass by. I try to remember to thank them for their beautiful songs and encouragement along the trail. I watch the lizards scurry and sometimes stop to flex with push-ups for me. Different times of the year bring different kinds of blooms—all wild and of all shapes and sizes. And when they grow in seemingly impossible circumstances, like out of rocks, I'm reminded that nothing is impossible with God. I adore the blue skies and sunshine, but when I get to be in the presence of God's puffy white clouds against those gorgeous hues of Arizona blues, my heart sings added praises. They just make me so happy!

On one cool spring morning, as I trod a soft dirt path around a mountain in my neighborhood, I was lost in deep conversation with God. I was talking to Him and sharing with Him that I felt like I'd had so much taken from me. *So much stolen.* Time, memories, money, my smile, my laugh, happiness, my health, and most importantly, my two oldest children. Even the closeness and stability in my marriage. Satan comes to steal. And he has stolen quite a lot from me.

What I didn't know was there was another season of loss just ahead.

As I continued my walk, I spoke to God about my older kids and reminded Him how much I love them and miss them. I knew He already knew. Still, I reminded Him that He had trusted me. He had trusted me enough to send them to me. He had picked me to be their mom. He had picked me to raise them and love them. I told Him how much of their lives I was missing out on and how sad and broken I was about all that I wasn't able to be a part of. I reminded Him of all the ways I was healing and forgiving and trying to lay it all at His feet, but I couldn't help but still feel the hurt. I still felt the persecution, the judgment, the betrayal, the shame, and the pain. All the suffering this season had piled on me and my life. I was feeling the sorrow in every new moment I didn't (and still don't) get to experience and cherish. It felt like I was missing out on a lot. And yes, it's true: I still live with the emptiness of going through seasons of life carrying this unexpected pain and sorrow. I knew He cared.

As tears poured down my cheeks with every dusty step I took, every word that passed through my lips, I could feel His presence. I knew He was there. I knew He was hearing me, completely exposed. No walls of protection.

Then I fell silent. I had no more words to share. He'd heard all I wanted to remind Him of. After some silence, I felt Him remind me of something: He is enough for me. He has and never will be taken from me. He will always and forever be right here with me. And in that moment, and in every other moment where I have felt completely alone, He was and is my portion. He is with me.

And He is with you. *Immanuel.*

> When humans and this world fail us, hurt us so much that we feel completely alone, please know that we are not alone.

He doesn't want us to do life alone. When humans and this world fail us, hurt us so much that we feel completely alone, please know that *we are not alone*. He wants us to come to Him and talk to Him so He can reassure us and love us the way only He can. Perfectly. He wants to lift us and carry us through. He wants to remind us of who we are to Him. When fear takes hold and we just don't know what's coming next, He reminds us not to fear. He is near to the brokenhearted. He is enough (Psalm 34:18).

"Fear thou not; for I am with thee: be not dismayed; for I am thy God: I will strengthen thee; yea, I will help thee; yea, I will uphold thee with the right hand of my righteousness" (Isaiah 41:10, KJV).

God promises to be close to the brokenhearted. That, my friend, doesn't mean everyone but you. It doesn't mean only if you feel like you deserve it. It doesn't mean only if you've never messed up and have deemed yourself worthy. It means, in your sorrow, in your hurting, He is right there with you. When it feels like the world is against you and nothing is going your way, He is there.

I've done a specific healing exercise several times, but the first time, I was instructed to visualize a particular emotionally devastating event—the day we went to court after twenty-one months without seeing, hugging, or sharing my life with my daughter and oldest son. I pictured myself in the courtroom with my husband Dylan behind me, my attorney beside me, and the judge before me. I visualized my ex-husband and the others. I saw the furniture with a pitcher of water and a box of tissues on the table. I recalled the nervousness, fear, and heartbreak I had felt in the original moments. This time, however, I was instructed to see Jesus sitting beside me, offering me comfort. Keeping me safe. Holding my hand and holding me up when I fell apart. Being present with me in every moment of the brokenness of this memory.

This, my friend, is a powerful visualization exercise and healing experience. To understand the truth that He is always, always, always there! In your most horrible and painful moments. He is there to bring you comfort.

This strategy reminds us that even when we feel most alone, we aren't, and He is enough. I invite you to be brave and visualize yourself back in those rooms of darkness, suffering, and pain, then invite Jesus to stand with you and fill that space with His light. Invite Him to come beside you so you can feel His presence and His peace in your hurting. Let's rewrite these narratives to empower us in our healing so He can do the thing in us that will allow us to stand tall and sing His praises! To be brave enough to let Him be our enough. To say yes to whatever He will call us to, to use this hardship that was meant to destroy us for good instead. He will use it, and we will hear Him say, "It is good!"

Chapter Five

Tearing Down the Walls

I was experiencing the loss of my children, but there was no funeral. My children were gone in what felt like an instant, but they were still living. I was grieving without end, and there seemed no way to begin the healing process. No turning of a page. No sense of closure.

Very few people knew I was suffering the loss of my children. Fewer knew the darkness in which I lived. Only those closest to me understood what was happening in our shattered world.

As is typical in the cases of death, there were no deliveries of hugs and casseroles. There were no stories shared of fun times or happy memories, no reminiscing when mourning friends and family stopped by to check in. The world didn't stop for me to have time to process all that I was going through. All that I was feeling. I didn't get to stay in my bed with my covers pulled up over my head and cry into the pain I was enduring.

The grieving wouldn't lessen. The raw heartbreak continued with each horrifying day. Every day, it was as if I'd lost them again. Over and over, the trauma replayed in my mind. There was no peace in knowing they were with Jesus. When there's no death but only loss, there is no promise of healing, safety, happiness, peace, or resting in the truth that they were snuggled close to their Savior, listening to His stories of travels and teachings. They weren't hearing His voice share about what the disciples did in their spare time when they weren't learning from or ministering with the Savior of the World.

My children were also suffering. They had lost their mother. I knew they were hurting, and I couldn't help them. I couldn't hold them. For the first time in their lives, I wasn't able to be Mom and comfort them and speak love and hope into them. At least I knew God had His arms wrapped around them. But I so desperately wanted to as well.

Fear on the Frontline

In addition to mourning the loss of my living children, I was in a nightmare battle for my life and for my children's right to have a relationship with both their parents. My marriage. My business. My reputation. They all suffered. I was being attacked and falsely accused of incredible things. Even people I'd never met attacked me; these were people I'd never even been in the same room with. I didn't even know their last names, but they came out as false witnesses against me. The battlefield was at my doorstep every single day. Some days worse than others. And the war raged on.

In those moments, when the pain of betrayal and falsehoods were so deep, I also felt the pain and suffering of those around me. Everyone else whom I loved was mourning the loss of my living children. They, like me, didn't get to say goodbye or give one last hug. They didn't get to tell my children how much they were loved. They didn't get to encourage them with words of hope. They were also caught off-guard. Those who knew us well knew everything had been suddenly torn apart. So I know those around us were hurting too. I could see it when they stared at me with disbelief, the visible ache of not knowing how to help plastered all over their faces. I could hear it in their shaky voices and see it in their parted lips when they were at a loss for words.

I also felt the weight of the heartbreak and sorrow for Dylan and our youngest boy, who were not only living this nightmare alongside me but also losing parts of me too. They lost the joy found in my soul, my smile, and my laugh. They endured those periods when I was locked in my prayer closet, sobbing alone and learning to survive this new life we never asked for. I was taking the time I needed to process and feel and trying not to put the weight of it all onto them, so I was "gone" in nearly every sense. I was paralyzed with fear. Fear for the next email, the next phone call, the next person to show up unexpectedly with more horror, or the next false accusation I would need to battle. Dylan and my son stared into the swollen eyes of so much heartbreak. They endured my quiet. They peered into a face that could barely remember how to smile. And when I could muster something up, I'm certain they could still find the pain behind my words or actions. I knew this was hurting them, too, but I couldn't make it stop. I felt like I couldn't help any of them, let alone myself.

In the early months, I was only able to survive, hour by hour.

The Relentless Replay

During this season of crisis, as we often do in our humanness, my mind re-ran all the events that had taken place. There were replays of conversations and moments I wished I could go back and somehow make different. Instead, I couldn't let them go. I wish I'd had the time to hold my daughter and son a lot longer, listen harder, and laugh and joke and play more. I'd remind them — every day — that I was their mom and that they get to love me and be loved by me. And that the latter was a fierce kind of love. I'd remind them that children need a mom and how blessed they were to have one who loves them so much—instead of my believing they already knew that.

Sometimes those regrets still replay. Friend, I imagine yours do for you too.

In seeking to figure out how to gain control over these replay horrors, to take back my mind and my control, I read books and listened to different pastors' sermons. In my younger years, I'd read or heard that if we memorized Bible verses, we could quickly bring up a verse to help us in our times of needed reassurance. To bring peace and hope back into our hearts. I'm sure you've heard this well-intentioned advice too.

I'm here to tell you that when these moments of horror played in my head, I could not, for the life of me, remember the Bible verses I'd memorized. I just couldn't recall them. And then I'd be frustrated and upset with myself, making the situation much worse. I'd ask myself what was wrong with me, and then this horrible cycle of pain and torture continued. When we're in emotional canyons like this, it's hard to pull facts or words from our brains. We must let the Holy Spirit direct.

I know God has given me control to choose my thoughts, actions, and reactions. I know His words are true. I trusted Him and believed His promises. I needed to take back my mind and focus on Him. But I was having the hardest time.

But God!

As the relentless cycle of negative thoughts weighed heavily on my heart, I prayed for the strength to overcome the crippling feeling I couldn't make stop. I desperately needed help. I felt inspired to listen to worship music every moment I could. Worship, specifically the music and singing, is my favorite part of a church service. There's not a church worship service I can get through without it bringing me to tears. Sometimes silent streams run down my cheeks as I sing His praises. And sometimes, I can't even get the words across my lips because I know that if the words are spoken aloud, the floodgates of emotion will flow.

So I obediently turned on worship music and listened as the musicians praised God through their lyrics. The music in my car was always on worship channels during this time. I listened to songs while I got myself ready in the morning at home. And in our clinic, where I worked, I submerged myself in worship music. I was in His Word through praise. It was then I noticed that when my mind returned to those painful moments, whether the initial loss of my children or the additional challenges, hurts, and loss that followed, I could quickly recall a song from memory and just sing! Often singing in my head, I could sing His praises, no matter where I was: working, working out, or at 2 a.m. when a painful dream woke me from an unrestful sleep. I could praise my Father in Heaven who loves me so much that He would answer my broken, pleading prayers with a blanket of comfort.

> "But as for me, afflicted and in pain—
> may your salvation, God, protect me.
> I will praise God's name in song and
> glorify him with thanksgiving"
> (Psalm 69:29-30).

Something I love about listening to worship music is there's always an uplifting and positive message. However, some songs are slower than others. Beautiful message or not, there's a time and place for the slow ones. I couldn't listen to many of the slow worship songs during those hardest times. I often needed a more upbeat tempo to lift me up! After all, I was attempting to live life as normally as possible, with most of the world not having a clue about what we were going through.

Skip.

Skip.

Skip.

That's what I did. I skipped the slower songs to get those that would lift my soul. What about you? Might you find some music that uplifts you?

The Art of Never

In Numbers 21:4-9, Moses and the people of Israel traveled through the wilderness on their way to the Promised Land. The Israelites started impatiently complaining to Moses about God's provision, or lack thereof, and asking if they'd been led there to die. They were discouraged and cranky, probably hungry and tired, and the Bible says their "soul loatheth this light bread" (verse 5) dining selection, with no water. They openly expressed their wish to Moses to return to Egypt, where they'd been enslaved but had meals instead of out in the wilderness, eating a continuous supply of mana.

God responded to the complaints by sending fiery serpents, which killed many. This drove the Israelites to repent, and they pleaded with Moses to ask the Lord to take away the serpents. Moses prayed and God told Moses to make a snake and put it up on a pole; anyone who is bitten can look at it and live. (Numbers 21:9)

> ... this story show us that being damaged doesn't mean we will stay damaged.

Obviously, we know it's not customary for us to heal from a snake bite by simply looking at a brass statue of the very thing that caused us pain and suffering. I think it was a lesson in faith, and I also think this story shows us that being damaged doesn't mean we will stay damaged.

We can heal. We just need a little faith—and probably some tears and some elbow grease.

What if we are called to face the thing we fear or what is hurting us as part of our healing? Just like God asked the Israelites to do?

At the beginning of my deep dive and saturation of Christian music into my life, to fill in and slowly plug up the gaping holes of my heart and soul, I received a court order to attend a class, and there was a short deadline to do so. It couldn't have happened any better than the exact way God needed me to go through it. However, I assure you, that's not what I was feeling at the time. Those were not the words coming out of my mouth. I was complaining just like the Israelites had been in the wilderness. And not just to God.

What made it worse was that there was only one class available during the deadline period, and the person causing my suffering had to attend the class with me! For several weeks, the two of us were forced to be in the same room for hours at a time. Feel me here: this was crazy heavy. It was painful. It was scary. My heart was ripped right open again and again each week. This was probably one of the hardest things I've ever had to do. To be seated in the same room with the person who had taken my children from me was certainly not in my plans. *Never.*

But God.

God had me "never-ing" like I had never "never-ed" before. I went into that room and faced my demon(s). Each day, I stared at the face responsible for my sobbing in my car just a few minutes before. Each day, I prayed for strength and to learn the lessons God needed me to learn in this place.

And every week, on my way to this class, I turned up my "Jesus music" so loud that I'm sure the cars around me could hear it. I'd sometimes sit in a panic, shaking like an autumn leaf, taking deep breaths, and hoping the words I heard through the speakers would seep into my soul. Sometimes, I'd belt out the words, praying I'd receive them. And then I'd arrive in the parking lot — early enough to ensure I had time to pray and fix my makeup afterward. I'd sit quietly in the car, with my head down, tears pouring down my cheeks, and I'd pray for strength. For peace. I didn't know why I needed to be in this situation, but I knew God had something He wanted me to learn from this.

What if we are called to face the thing we fear as part of our healing? What if it's a lesson in faith that we're going to be okay? I mean, I didn't die. I'm here writing this account. Maybe I'm calling the experience a blessing.

> God had me all along.

To this day, I believe the Lord was teaching me that I was safe and held by Him. I could face the thing I feared the most. In this situation, I could face the person I feared the most. That even in the same room, he couldn't hurt me. God had me all along. And even though this person was causing me more pain and suffering than I ever thought I could live through, I was still functioning. I was still breathing. God still had me — He always has me — and He loves me immeasurably. He has a purpose for me, even though I couldn't see it then. I would have given my everything to have my old life back, talking and laughing and being with all of my children like normal, to have everything the way it was. I was terrified I'd never get that back. The unknown: that's the scariest place.

One week, God reaffirmed I was safe with Him. As I was driving to class, He brought me yet another beautiful lesson. A lesson of just how loved I am came pouring through my car speakers and filling my weary and afraid heart. In His perfect timing, He delivered the song "You Are Loved," by Stars Go Dim! It was His reminder that despite all that was going on in my life, despite the hard moments, despite all I was enduring, all I needed to do was look up because the One who loves me unconditionally was always there. *Is* always there. In my hurting, in my healing. Through it all. He loves me! And friend, He adores you too!

After I arrived at the parking lot and turned off the radio, as I did each week before class and prayed, I turned the radio back on and the radio DJ announced that Stars Go Dim would be playing a concert in a small church near my home that very evening! I knew I needed to be there in that chapel, to feel the Holy Spirit fill and lift my soul.

I called Dylan and told him what had happened and that we'd be going to the concert that evening. Another miracle that transpired is that our youngest son just happened *not* to have soccer practice that evening. It had been canceled — a miracle! — and our calendar was cleared in a God-sized way. We went to the private concert, and it was beautiful! Well, not my sobby self. But everything else was. What a night! What a memory of God's presence and His continuous gift of everything we needed in the right moment we needed it.

Oh, how worship music speaks to my soul. What a beautiful blessing our loving Father has given us to connect with Him. Worship, our direct lifeline to the One who will always love us, no matter what season or place we are in. We can praise Him in our joy, and we can praise Him in our suffering.

In the Arms of His Love

Romans 5:3-5, in the KJV, says, "And not only so, but we glory in tribulations also: knowing that tribulation worketh patience; and patience, experience; and experience, hope: a hope maketh not ashamed; because the love of God is shed abroad in our hearts by the Holy Ghost which is given unto us." To summarize, tribulation brings patience. Patience brings experience. Experience brings hope. And in all of this, our hope is in our God who loves us so!

There's something to learn in this place. Something new.

What if being so broken, shattered beyond recognition—even pulverized to dust—is the exact thing we must experience to understand God's love and the fullness of who He is and how much He adores us?

What if He's using our horrible, harder-than-we-ever-thought-we-could-survive thing to bring us back to or closer to Him?

For a long time, I was convinced the brokenness, the dust, was the end. That I'd always be broken, never be whole again. Maybe I'd never feel joy again. Or laugh or play again. But what if our brokenness is really the beginning? What if I trusted Him enough to let Him put me back together? What if I trusted that He would make me new? What if I trusted that He would use this really bad thing for good? And what about you, friend? What if?

> "So do not fear, for I am with you; do not be dismayed, for I am your God. I will strengthen you and help you; I will uphold you with my righteous right hand" (Isaiah 41:10).

I have felt Him hold me. I know He has carried me through every one of these hard moments. And I'm certain that when I experienced moments that weren't so hard, that was Him too, making the way a little less troublesome.

On one particularly rough night, when my mind kept torturing me and I seemed unable to take back control while lying on my tear-soaked pillow, I rolled away from my sleeping husband, trying not to wake him. I hoped I'd just peacefully fall back to sleep while I was praying. I asked God to let me feel His arms wrapped around me. I felt so alone. The sorrow was too much to bear. I pleaded through silent sobs that He would "please, please, please" just wrap His arms around me and show me He was really there.

Friend, what followed was one of the most amazing feelings I've ever felt. I sensed Him wrap His arms around me. I felt the pressure and the tightness of His loving embrace. His peace seeped into every cell of my body, and it was pure magic.

> "My flesh and my heart faileth: But God is the strength of my heart, and my portion for ever" (Psalm 73:26, KJV).

Can we sing a hallelujah right here together?! I sing a hallelujah!!!

He will be our strength, as long as we let Him.

One of my favorite things I've learned from sermons, devotions, and personal study is to talk to Him—and as much as possible. All the days of my life! He is our Father. And He loves us and wants to have an intimate relationship with us. He wants us to bring every detail of our lives to Him. Good and bad. Happy and sad. Little and big. And I love talking with Him. I especially love when I'm going through something and feel overwhelmed, stressed, hurting, or even excited and happy, and the Holy Spirit reminds me to talk to our Father, sharing whatever it is I'm going through with Him. I love the promptings! And I love it more when I listen (wink).

> *"Rejoice evermore. Pray without ceasing. In every thing give thanks: for this is the will of God in Christ Jesus concerning you"* (1 Thessalonians 5:16-18, KJV).

I was many months into my battle, and my heart was weary from the long-suffering. As I was driving in the car on my way to work, I had the music turned off and was talking to God. Traffic was heavy, but we were moving at a steady pace. The skies were a gorgeous blue, as they often are here in the Valley of the Sun. I was basking in God's presence and just enjoying a great commute conversation with Him. I don't recall what we were talking about, but I do remember looking over to my right, and the car just ahead had a license plate that read ITSGOOD. At that moment, I smiled, tears welling up in my eyes. He reminded me I was going to be okay. He speaks to us in fun ways. And when we spend more time with Him, we can recognize when He puts things right in front of us to tell us what we need in that particular moment. And that moment certainly was good.

Chapter Six

Renewed in the Ruins

I lie in bed, warm, safe, and comfortable. Tears pour down and are soaked up in the softness of my pillowcase. Sobs well up in my chest, threatening to explode. My heart is so broken, and I feel like it'll never stop—like I'll never recover. I feel like the torture is never-ending, and I just don't have the strength to keep fighting this war that I don't think I should ever have had to fight. The battle rages on, and I'm growing more exhausted, more depleted, and more hopeless day by day. The me that was is disappearing. I'm feeling the pain of a mother's heart that aches and longs to hold her children again. The burning need to tell them I'm so sorry they're in this place and that I'm going to make things right. I'll just want to protect them and mend their brokenness.

But I can't.

I'm suffering rejection from my children, the ones I'd lay down my own life for. A man who used to love me is now keeping them from me, and they were the only things I ever wanted in this life. I'm facing rejection from family who know me, who I believed loved me and would never hurt me; rejection from strangers I've never met, standing so firmly in support of my judgment; persecution—all based on lies.

It feels like too much to bear.

I'm lying here wide awake, living through Hell. My worst nightmare has come true, and I'm forced to watch helplessly, wait, and feel every single second of this awful torture. In the stillness and quiet of the night, my mind reminds me of all I've been through. Over and over. And the pain is so much, it boils up and just flows down my cheeks in constant streams.

I hear Dylan open our bedroom door and quietly, on bare feet, cross our bedroom floor. He gently pulls back the covers and tenderly climbs in beside me. It doesn't take long for him to realize I'm lying awake in my suffering, even though I'm trying hard to keep it from him. He scooches over and pulls me to his warm chest. He wraps me up in his arms and holds me. No words. Just comfort. Just love. It's a silent acknowledgment of what I'm facing: the horrific pain and sorrow — all that I'm feeling.

He also knows my days have turned into nights with the neverending darkness. There is a pain that doesn't leave when the sun comes up. The battle remains. The darkness remains. The emptiness sits so heavy on my heart.

> "If you try and ignore your sadness, it just finds a way to leak out of you anyway." — Eleanor Shellstrop, *The Good Place*

As much as I hope and pray for it, this nightmare isn't one I'm waking up from. And who knows if I ever will. Well, God knows. Meanwhile, I am forced to watch it unfold moment by moment, day by day, night by night.

I can't seem to make any sort of positive change or save myself, let alone them. I can't move. I can't breathe. I'm completely stuck in this moment, and nothing I do makes it better. The waiting is such a hard place to be in. I'm a doer. I want to do something and get somewhere. I want to fix this thing that's gone so wrong. I want to be in control of the now and the next. Waiting and being out of control are two difficult places for me to sit. I don't care for them much.

I imagine you can relate.

Friend, I know you're exhausted too. I can remember how exhausted I was in those first dark chapters. My heart is with you, and I want to take this moment to remind you that God loves you. He sees you hurting; He sees your pain; He knows you're tired. He knows you're off balance, and He knows you feel like you can't take one more vicious blow.

I am also here with you. We are going to move through this chapter of suffering together. And friend, I'm so sorry for what you are going through.

Remember the story of Elijah and how he suffered through so much? He spent many years in hiding, running for his life. He endured years of drought. He went up against King Ahab to prove that the Canaanite gods were not the one true God, and he even poked the bear by having all the priests of Baal killed. Jezebel planned to kill him, and then Elijah ran for his life.

In 1 Kings 19:4–8, we learn Elijah, exhausted from suffering so much and for so long, travels a day's journey into the wilderness. He sits under a juniper tree and prays, telling God he's had enough. He is tired and weary and just done. Put-a-fork-in-him done. I imagine you can relate? I know I sure do. Elijah asks God to just let him die. Then, after making this very final request, Elijah lies down and takes a nap. How does God respond? As Elijah naps, God sends an angel who touches Elijah and wakes him up. The angel has bread and water and instructs him to rise and eat. Elijah eats and drinks, and then, with a full belly, he lies back down for another nap. Elijah is literally instructed to eat, drink, and then take another nap! God sends the angel *again* to instruct Elijah to eat and drink once more "because the journey is too great" (verse 7).

A big lesson we can take from Elijah's story is that we must eat and nourish ourselves for our journey. We must hydrate, and we must sleep. It's all part of our healing. This journey you and I are on— it's a big journey, and we need to take care of ourselves through it.

Please hear me. Sometimes, we just need to drink a glass of cold water, eat something nourishing, and climb into our comfy, cozy, warm, safe bed to just *be*. A nap may not come, but the rest will do us good even if we can't sleep. We can pray. We can let our Father calm our minds and bring us peace.

And let me also say this: you must get back up! Elijah got back up and went back out on his journey. It's okay to take a minute and feel and cry and purge your pain. You have to release it. And this may happen over and over. It's part of the healing journey. But, sweetheart, you have to get up! God is going to use you. He is going to use your story of suffering. So you can't stay there in that hard place. You must get up!

God Is Not the Storm

God spoke to Elijah: "And he said, Go forth, and stand upon the mount before the Lord. And, behold, the Lord passed by, and a great and strong wind rent the mountains, and brake in pieces the rocks before the Lord; but the Lord was not in the wind: and after the wind an earthquake; but the Lord was not in the earthquake: And after the earthquake, a fire; but the Lord was not in the fire: and after the fire a still small voice. And it was so, when Elijah heard it, that he wrapped his face in his mantle, and went out, and stood in the entering in of the cave. And, behold, there came a voice unto him, and said, What doest thou here, Elijah?" (1 Kings 19:11-13, KJV).

God is not the storm you're facing. This pain and suffering that you're enduring, He did not send this to you. He is not causing it. This pain and suffering is because we live in the brokenness between two perfect gardens.

> ...the Father is not the storm, and He is not in the storm.

From Mark 4:35-41: Remember when Jesus and His disciples left the crowd behind, got into a boat, and sailed out? Jesus was peacefully asleep in the stern of the boat, lying on a cushion. Can you see it? The boat is thrashing about in giant waves. I'd be throwing up! So this massive storm is raging, and Jesus is sound asleep, not worrying about anything, not sick or throwing up. Why? Because He trusts the Father, and He knows the Father is not the storm and is not *in* this storm. This is important right here: *The Father is not the storm, and He is not in the storm.*

The disciples freak out and run to Jesus and wake Him up, asking. "Don't you care if we drown?" Jesus stands up. Can you imagine how calm He is? I can see it all in my mind. I can't wait to be with Him and hear him tell the story, though. Jesus just casually stands up, rebukes the wind, and says to the waves, "Quiet! Be still!" And guess what happens? You already know! They obey! The wind and waves calm right down. Jesus would never tell our Heavenly Father to be quiet! That's because Jesus knows the Father is not the storm and is not in the storm. And Jesus certainly has the power to command the storm. So He did! The storm, not the Father.

This story reminds me that even though we go through storms—and sometimes these storms are large enough to knock us so far off-balance that it's hard to get grounded again, and they're so dark and dreary that we cannot see—we have to remember that it's not God's storm. But also remember that He is always with us in the storm. He's here right beside us, bringing us peace and carrying us when our feet are too wobbly for us to carry ourselves.

Your Father in Heaven loves you immensely! And I know He isn't your storm. He isn't in your earthquake or the winds that take the very breath out of your lungs. He isn't what is breaking you to unrecognizable pieces. He isn't the fiery flames in which you stand. He didn't cause this *thing*. But please know that He most certainly knows what you're going through, and He is with you. He is with you in every second. With every broken piece. And if you've been here in this place for a while, maybe, He's saying to you, "What are you doing here? Beloved child, you can't stay here. You must get up. Your story doesn't stop here. This is not the end! It is not finished."

I have often found myself saying, "It's not supposed to be this way." This isn't the story I wrote for myself. This isn't my fairytale life, my "Happily Ever After." It should have, could have been so very different. It was supposed to be different. I guess I thought other people would go through hard things but that I could control every aspect of my life and avoid the hard things. I believed my life would turn out just how I had always planned and imagined it would. All happy and floaty, like white puffy clouds across the most perfect blue sky. Just magical and lovely. Sparkles and rainbows and constant joy-filled moments.

But I don't have control over all the things, certainly not what's happened to me. And neither do you. But we do have control over getting up. We have control over our healing, growing, and living. We have control over listening to the guidance and direction God gives us. We can listen to the whisper He often provides. That's where He's at. He isn't the storm, but we can use this pain to run to Him. He's part of the healing, of the entire journey to help others. We can use this thing that broke us to dust and praise the Father who got us through it.

Because, friend, we must get through it. We can learn to glorify Him in every minute of our struggle, our healing, and our victory! And since it's not done—because it's not good yet—remember, there will be victory! We will see the Victory, who is Christ! We will see the goodness of God in this thing!

> "And the God of all grace, who called you to his eternal glory in Christ, after you have suffered a little while, will himself restore you and make you strong, firm and steadfast" (1 Peter 5:10).

I'm pretty sure you've suffered, maybe for a long while. I know you have because you're here with me now, and I can assure you that I've suffered for a very long while too. But let's allow Him to make us perfect. Let's let Him re-establish us. Let's let Him give us strength and settle us because, oh boy, He's got work for us to do!

> "'For I know the plans I have for you,' declares the LORD, 'plans to prosper you and not to harm you, plans to give you hope and a future. Then you will call on me and come and pray to me, and I will listen to you. You will seek me and find me when you seek me with all your heart. I will be found by you,' declares the LORD, 'and will bring you back from captivity . . .'" (Jeremiah 29:11-14).

In the next bit of this passage, God says He will bring you back from all the places where you were banished and carried into exile. Let's sit here for a minute. Because if you've endured similar rejection, betrayal, persecution, and horribly untrue judgments as I have, doesn't that just light a flame in your heart?! God is promising so much in these words. He knows His plans for you, and all of those horrible things that happened to you can't stop Him! He has plans to bring you back! To restore all that was lost or stolen. He has plans to prosper you and give you an oh-so-beautiful future.

The Weight of What Should Have Been

> We need to release control and let Him do His thing. We must listen when He whispers and move when He says move.

Maybe this is where we should do a deeper dive into releasing the idea of what we thought our life should be like. This has been a treacherous space for me. I harbored images of my life and future, and I'd always had the perception of control. I had to realize these promises God offers may require us to give up that control we grip so tightly. We must place our trust in Him with our entire lives, our futures, and every plan we have to get there. We can't hold on to that control and vision of what we thought our life should be like while, at the same time, hoping for His promised future. We just can't have both control and release. We need to release control and let Him do His thing. We must listen when He whispers and move when He says move.

We can find and rest in hope in His promises for our future. The one He has planned for us! He promises to bring us back out of this captivity and the brokenness we've been living in. He will bring us out of those dark nights that seem never-ending—and leave us drifting off at night with tears in our eyes—and into the light. He'll give us rest from the exhaustion of fighting for every breath and every broken heartbeat.

God is coming for us!!! He wants to bring us back to Him. "Call on me. Pray to me and I will listen. Seek me with all your heart." — Your loving Father (paraphrased from Jeremiah 29:12-13).

The Gift of Rejection

Rejection positions us for our purpose. Stick with me here. I don't—and I imagine you don't either—feel like rejection is a gift. Maybe, at best, it's an unwanted gift. Like a vacuum from your husband on your birthday. So this idea may take some time to process. But here we are, sitting in this hard place, trying to see the good in it. We're healing and growing, looking for the light in the darkest of days. God is calling us to a purpose. We aren't here to simply suffer, endure, and repeat. That's a horrible cycle of existing. But I believe suffering itself is part of our healing journey to figure out what our purpose is. We can pray, fast, and meditate on our role in our pain, and if there's anything we need to heal or correct, we can repent or apologize for it. Now's a great time for that. After all, we must still do our part.

But what if another purpose is to draw closer to God? Or maybe it's to learn He is real? What if it's to learn to talk to Him more? To trust Him more? To rely on Him and not on our understanding or on the broken world and people around us? What if the purpose is to bring us to His Word to find His Truth for ourselves?

What if this rejection can anchor our identity in Jesus? And what if Jesus can bring us the freedom we need from the very thing that brought us to Him in the first place?

In my brokenness, I studied and pored over Job's story. I can relate to many aspects of his suffering. I can't wait to sit with God and talk to Him about all that I've experienced in this broken garden. I can't wait to hear what He saw and learn what He was doing behind the scenes, through it all, just like Job.

I've had so many things in life taken from me. From people I loved (and still do! Very much.) to possessions I cherished, and even money I've earned. I didn't have a tight grip on the money and things; when they were gone, I healed from those losses pretty quickly. I know God's got me; He's taking care of my needs, and He will always provide. But those people I love deeply, with my whole being, I definitely have a tight grip on them. And I really feel their loss deep in my soul.

Because of that kind of loss, I have lived in uncertainty. *What's next?* I wonder daily. *What will my future look like?* I live in the unknown of if my life will always be like it is now. Should I just get used to this? Will I get to enjoy life with my children and grandchildren someday? Will I get to travel and have experiences and make memories with those I love most? Will I get to enjoy any of the dreams I have held? Will anything ever be as I had hoped it would? Will I ever smile and not feel guilty?

Or does the future look completely different? Completely new?

Whatever the outcome, I have faith. And hope.

I believe things can change and that all my dreams can still be realized. Even if they look different from what I previously thought. I have faith that God will deliver on His promises. I trust in His words. But unlike my studies of the book of Job, I can't turn a few pages and see how God will show up or how He's working behind the scenes. I can't see what the amazing and beautiful ending looks like for my story, not right now. I can't yet see that everything comes together, way better than I could have ever imagined it on my own. That His plan is the best plan.

I trust in the Lord, but even though I trust Him fully, sometimes the pain causes me to doubt whether His promises are truly for me. When He promises rest, peace, joy, and restoration, will I have that too? He's promised He has amazing and wonderful things planned. Sometimes I wonder if those are for everyone else? Everyone but me . . .

If you're thinking the same thing, let's remember this little gem: "Before I formed you in the womb I knew you, before you were born I set you apart" (Jeremiah 1:5).

He knows you and loves you. He knows me and loves me. All of His promises and blessings are for both of us! Not just everyone else. And He wants us to turn to Him. To rely on Him. He doesn't expect us to handle all of our pain and brokenness on our own. He doesn't want us to rely on our strength but instead rely on His.

Pray. Seek. Call on me. I will listen. I will be found (paraphrased from Jeremiah 29:12-14).

"Blessed are those who are persecuted because of righteousness, for theirs is the kingdom of heaven" (Matthew 5:10).

"Blessed are ye, when men shall revile you, and persecute you, and shall say all manner of evil against you falsely, for my sake. Rejoice, and be exceeding

> glad: for great is your reward in heaven: for so persecuted they the prophets which were before you" (Matthew 5:11-12, KJV).

Hold on to these precious promises. Let them seep into your soul and fill you up with God's love! God's got you!

Chapter Seven

In the Arms of My Refuge

I saw tears and swollen, puffy eyes and a face that didn't even look like me anymore staring back as I stood hypnotically gazing into my large bathroom mirror. I saw pain and bewilderment. And frustration, fear, and disbelief. I saw suffering. I didn't see God moving. I didn't see Him making it right or even any better. He didn't wave His arm or say a word like I know He can to make all the craziness disappear. He didn't bring my babies back. He didn't bring my other family back. He didn't stop the fight, the persecution, or the continual attacks on my husband, my family, me, our business — my entire life. Instead, the torment grew worse with each passing day.

At least, that's what my emotions were screaming. God wasn't doing His part!

My emotions are not true. They are real and valid but not true.

Trusting God is a daily practice, especially in this extreme level of brokenness. In the loss of my children, the battle fighting to be their mom again in every sense of the word, and all the other events that surrounded this chapter of my life swirled around me. I'm not here asking you to do this alone. I'm not saying that trusting God comes naturally. Or easily. I'm not saying you won't have moments where you pull off into a grocery store parking lot because the tears won't stop flowing, and you can't see well enough to keep yourself and those around you safe while driving. Where you, safely parked, proceed to scream at the top of your lungs. And with pleading sobs of "Why?!" completely fall apart right there. It may happen. God is not asking you to pull it together and then come to Him. He's asking you to come to Him first, as you are falling apart, in the middle of the crazy. That's it. Coming to Him is the obedience I believe He's looking for.

God is there, in the chaos! Find Him! Choose Him!

> The only way to gain unwavering faith and trust in God is to survive and thrive, to go through it.

Obedience is trusting God to act in ways our feelings may not agree. The only way to gain unwavering faith and trust in God is to survive and thrive, to go through it.

To go through the suffering and the pain. Through all the hard things. Through the chaos. Through the mess.

Going through our suffering often makes us question God. We might doubt His goodness, love, or truth. And that's why we are here together right now. That's why, with the pile of snotty and tear-soaked tissues in our laps and the next cool glass of water ready for us to rehydrate with, we are going to get to the thriving part. Together, we are going to do it. We are going to stand hand-in-hand, arms raised high above our heads, and celebrate that the enemy didn't get us! We will proclaim praises at all God does and will do—even when it's still messy. Even though it's not over yet. Even though we are in this moment, learning how to survive. We, together, my beautiful and worthy friend, will learn together how to thrive!

I'm stepping in with some real heart truth right here. Even though I'd much rather God wipe it all away with one beautiful swoop of His arm (or Jesus coming and flipping the table would be good too)—because that would be so much easier than going through all the pain and suffering—I trust that there's no better time than His timing. There's no better way than His way. And if you're still in the messy in-between with me, that idea might just take your breath away a little bit because it's hard to accept. And that's okay. I've been there too.

You don't have to be completely on board with the truth that His timing is the best. I have moments when I bounce in and out of that belief, too, because I just want what I want. And I don't think I'm really asking for that much. Plus, He gave me what I wanted, and now it's gone! So that is . . . really what He wants. Right? For me, I had to get back to, "Father, Your will be done. Thank You for giving me my minute."

I have spent so much time worrying. I have often sat, hid, and sulked in this ugly cloak of despair, worrying about what's coming next. I worry about meeting new people and how much of my authentic self they can handle. Is my real story too much to share, or is it too heavy for people to hear? Will it cause them to avoid me—or will it be a trigger and cause pain for them? Will they think I'm crazy? I worry about my health and the sickness the trauma has caused. I often hope I'll fully heal. And I wonder if I'll have good memories and smile at recalling them instead of only feeling loss and longing. Friend, I'm sure you're adding to the list as you read, and I'm certain, together, we could go on and on.

But . . .

We're getting caught up in what we thought our life would be like. We are living in our past: our past hopes, our past dreams, and our past hurts and sorrow. We're projecting all of that pain and suffering onto our future. We are stuck in this desperate in-between. It's holding us back, keeping us hostage in the idea of what our life should have been. What we thought it would be like. Our previous hopes and dreams. In the "It wasn't supposed to be this way" mentality.

This is the enemy. This is his nagging. This is us allowing him to control us. He is stealing our joy. He is stealing our future. He is stealing us from those who are in our lives right now, loving us and making memories with us today. He is stealing the *present*. He is making us focus on the "what should have beens" and the "what isn't." And it's a sucker punch to the gut—the *what* that may never be. We must lay the *what may never be* at the feet of God.

When we worry, we are in a perpetual state of fear. We read in Matthew 6:34 not to worry about what the future may hold. We should let it be until it becomes necessary to deal with it. And for that matter, *if* we ever need to deal with it. This not only includes the things we worry about but also the things we expect and hope for. How this speaks most to me is that I don't have to worry about the future. I guess my "worry" is more of a strong hope for what I *want* everything to look like and how I *want* it to turn out.

What a great reminder this is to be in the moment. This day, right here. Our Father has blessed us with so much. Even in the hurt. Even in the brokenness. Even in the unknown and the wanting. We have so much that we can just sit in the blessedness of the present as His beloved. In the abundance of all that He has provided for us.

Sheltered in Truth

It is in these times of worry that we must find our refuge. We can sit with God and let Him refresh and renew our souls. Remember when Jesus met Martha, going to visit with her and her sister Mary at their home? Miss Mary sat at Jesus's feet and soaked in all that He was saying. Miss Martha, on the other hand, was distracted, worrying about everything she thought needed to be done for Jesus during His visit. Martha believed Mary should be participating in all the things, including the worrying and the hurrying. She didn't feel it was the time to be sitting. Mary knew, though, that being present in this precious and perfect moment with Jesus was exactly where she wanted and needed to be.

Jesus says to her, "Martha, Martha" — hold up! He must have really wanted to get her attention if He's saying her name twice. I think this may be similar to when we say our children's full names (middle name included) in those moments when we really want them to pay attention. Maybe she needed the repetition to grab her attention from her mind-consuming worry?

"Martha, Martha, thou art careful and troubled about many things: But one thing is needful: and Mary hath chosen that good part, which shall not be taken away from her" (Luke 10:38-42, KJV).

Let's unpack a couple of the important parts of this passage. I want us to carry this forward, tucked inside of our hearts. Martha, Jesus says, was careful and troubled about many things. She was taking great care and precision in her tasks. She clearly had a love for Jesus, and she was worrying about making things just right for Him. She was probably trying extra hard to make things perfect. I can relate. If Jesus was physically here, I'd want to make sure the house was in order and all of His needs were met, that He was comfortable and well-fed. Wanting the conditions to be right for Jesus is not a bad thing, but we don't need the conditions right to be with Him.

We don't need to make sure the dishes are clean, we are showered, and we have our Bibles in hand to come to Him and talk with Him, to be in His presence and feel His peace. We can come as we are—hot mess and all, with chaos swirling around us. Tears? Okay. Angry? You bet. Joy and laughter? Yep! He wants it all! Just rest at His feet as Mary did.

And then, Jesus says to Martha, "Mary hath chosen that good part, which shall not be taken away from her" (Luke 10:42, KJV). Our rest is in Jesus. Our refuge is found in His love and will not be taken from us. It's here for us now. We must choose to sit, listen, release the worry and stress, and be present right now. We are needful of His peace. We are needful in this moment. And our need isn't to keep spinning in worry about what may or may never come about. We must be obedient. This is the lesson of Mary. She chose the good part—the part that cannot be taken from us. The good part is time in His presence. In Him! (Matthew 11:30).

Yes, sweet friend, there are tears and heartaches. No doubt. But I feel God is teaching us to look at so much more. He loves us and is blessing us in all that we are going through. We must trust

Him with the unknown and bask in the known. We must enjoy the moments we are blessed with each day and be thankful, for they're all precious gifts—even if they look different from what we expected.

The goodness of God shall not be taken from us. We just need to remember. To come find rest in Him. He is present with us. He is here to help us release control. I strongly believe that worry is our way of trying to hold on to control. And we can release it to God because the truth is there is so much out of our control.

The Promise of Peace

"Even though Jesus was God's Son, He learned obedience from the things He suffered," it says in Hebrews 5:8, in the NLT. Jesus learned obedience in His life here on earth—and on the cross. Our Father in Heaven asked Jesus to do these things (take on flesh and give up His life), and out of obedience, Jesus did them. He was betrayed and then beaten within a breath of life. He was a bloody and broken mess. He carried His own cross through town while being mocked. And then, nailed to a cross, hung until death. That's a whole lot of obedience. He fulfilled His promise to the Father to secure our salvation. It wasn't just at the beginning and the end, though. We see the obedience of Jesus throughout His entire life. He suffered temptation while fasting for forty days and dealt with the devil directly during that time (Matthew 4:1-11). He loved us before He came to earth in flesh, for His thirty-three years on earth, and still does today while sitting at the right hand of the Father, awaiting our return.

When Jesus ascended to Heaven, He left us His peace. He doesn't need it in Heaven, in the glory of God, so He left it here—for you and for me. "Peace I leave with you, my peace I give unto you: not as the world giveth, give I unto you. Let not your heart be troubled, neither let it be afraid" (John 14:27, KJV). We can receive that peace today!

Faith over Facts

When Jesus and the apostles traveled over Galilee, a huge crowd followed them because they had seen many of the miracles Jesus had performed. Jesus and the disciples went up a mountain to talk about how they were going to feed so many people. Spoiler alert: Jesus already knew what He was going to do, and I love that He was including His proteges in the plan even though He already had it all figured out. He has such a way of setting up the story. My heart smiles so much at this. Anyway, Simon tells Jesus there's a boy with five barley loaves and two small fish, assuring Jesus there was no way it would feed everyone. Jesus instructed them to have the five thousand men in attendance sit in the large grassy field, and then Jesus prayed a prayer of thanksgiving over the fish and bread and sent the disciples to distribute all they had. In the end, all of them—all five thousand men and who knows how many women and children—ate until they were full. And they still had leftovers! Twelve baskets full!

> **The enemy uses facts to convince us not to trust God's Word. Not to trust God's promises. Or His love for us.**

The enemy uses facts to convince us not to trust God's Word. Not to trust God's promises. Or His love for us.

Yet God always creates something out of nothing. Miracles are His domain. Satan twists and turns the truth to keep us deflated and defeated, which keeps us from our promised blessings. Thankfully, God's provision is limitless. Facts don't tell the whole story. Worldly facts said there was no way for the fish and loaves of bread to feed all of those people. That's a fact.

But God . . .

What worldly facts are keeping you stuck? What facts are keeping you in heartbreak, pain, sickness, and suffering? What earthly facts are blocking God's blessings? Satan uses facts to hold us down. To keep us stuck, unable or unwilling to move forward. When that happens, we're not receiving God's blessings. We're not doing what we're supposed to be doing—what we're being called to do. Stuck. Satan is keeping us from glorifying God.

Many of us are still in the in-between of our stories—between the incident that broke us and where our happy futures lie. We are still in the messy middle and enduring the pain. That is our fact. And hopefully, we're believing God for our miracle too. Because facts have nothing to do with faith.

> *Speak faith, not facts. Trust in the unseen. Expect what you haven't yet experienced.*

Speak faith, not facts. Trust in the unseen. Expect what you haven't yet experienced.

> *"For God hath not given us the spirit of fear; but of power, and of love, and of a sound mind" (2 Timothy 1:7, KJV).*

It's true: God rules by faith. The devil rules by fear.

> "Casting down imaginations, and every high thing that exalteth itself against the knowledge of God, and bringing into captivity every thought to the obedience of Christ" (2 Corinthians 10:5, KJV).

My friend, we must, in this place of in-between, take every negative, painful, exhausting, belittling, rejecting, untrue thought captive. We must change our thoughts to God's message of love for us. We must learn His truth so we can speak it over ourselves and block out the enemy's lies. We must learn to see ourselves through God's eyes. We must learn to not live in borrowed trouble. What I mean is all of these untrue negative things we tell ourselves are borrowed trouble from the evil one. They are not for us. We were never supposed to carry those horrible things with us.

It is time for us to find joy in releasing our worries.

As Exodus 33:14 says, "My Presence will go with you, and I will give you rest." God promised Moses this when He asked Moses to trust Him. And He is promising this to you too!

> *"Casting all your care upon him; for he careth for you"* (1 Peter 5:7, KJV).

Daddy's Job

When my youngest son approached the time of getting his driver's license, we helped him buy a safe used car. One of the things we really wanted to come out of this car was life experience. We wanted him to learn how to save money, including after the purchase itself, for unexpected repairs. We wanted him to learn to drive safely, so we made sure he had great instruction and extra classes. We wanted him to learn new skills, including researching issues the car had, the recommended parts, and how to make those repairs. We wanted him to have hands-on application and learning experiences.

There were also fun things to learn, like buying and installing new radios and speakers and building subwoofer boxes. The repairs and radio things didn't involve me. I'm not that kind of mom. I'm more the baking-cookies-in-the-kitchen mother—for when the repairs are finished—or the bringing-out-cold-water-to-keep-them-going mom. I am super blessed to have a husband who loves this boy like a biological son. He has always done all the "dad things" with the kids. And these mechanical and audio projects are certainly "daddy jobs" in my book!

The two of them often worked on the car together in the garage, getting greasy, making memories, and teaching and learning lifelong skills. Many frustrations unfolded in the garage and countless trips to the auto parts store were had. There were also laughing and joking around, and a bond, a closeness, was built in that space.

In life, when we face these hard times, the ones we didn't ask for, the painful ones, the ones that don't make sense at all, that are completely out of our control—these are the "Daddy jobs" (with a capital *D*). When we can't fix it or change it, we have a Father who can. We have a Daddy who will comfort and direct. In our hard moments, we need to remember God's job. We must give it all to Him, our mighty Daddy. So stop worrying. Stop trying to control the situation. Stop stressing. Just give it to Him.

Detours Ahead

One of our favorite family activities was taking trips in our RV. We loved going camping in the forest or going to the sand dunes. We took trips through multiple states and have seen landmarks, amazing forests, rivers, and oceans. We loved visiting family and friends all over the West Coast, and our RV allowed us to make and keep incredible memories.

On several of these trips, we experienced flat tires. When you're dealing with a flat tire on a car, it's not too big of a deal. You just change it quickly and get right back on the road. But when the flat tire is on a forty-two-foot-long fifth wheel or the truck pulling it, it's a little more of a *situation*. On one particular trip, Dylan and I were on our way to Oceanside, California, for a conference he was attending. About an hour outside of Yuma, Arizona, our tire sensor beeped at us. We'd gotten these tire sensors after several other flat tire stories I could share that would certainly be entertaining but don't quite fit my point here. So the sensor started beeping, and Dylan pulled off to the side of the highway to check it out. The tire looked fine but was a little low on air. He filled it up with the air compressor that he was smart enough to have installed on the RV, and we were back on the road. About ten minutes later, the sensor beeped again. And again, we pulled off. The tire was fine, just a little low again. We rinsed and repeated and got back on the road. This routine continued every ten minutes for an hour! At that point, I got on my phone, looking for a tire store in Yuma to figure out what the heck was going on.

We arrived in Yuma, parked the fifth wheel, left the truck with a service technician, and grabbed an early dinner while we waited, since we would arrive in California much later than expected. A phone call came in that the tire was just fine, but three tiny holes in the rim were creating a slow leak. They couldn't fix the rim and didn't have a new rim for us to purchase. But they put on the spare, and with full tummies and gratitude for our spare tire and prayers for safety on our travels, we were back on the road.

Friend, when we get a flat tire, do we let that moment ruin our lives for many years later, keeping us stranded and alone on the side of the road? Or do we get out, change the tire, get back on the road, and keep going?

This experience of feeling broken down on the side of the road that we find ourselves in now is only a few minutes (okay, days or months) on our entire journey. Yes, it's uncomfortable. Probably even hot and miserable. There will be some frustration and anger and maybe some words we wouldn't otherwise say out loud. And working through our broken-down condition is going to take longer than a blown tire on the side of a busy highway. It may be many years without an end in sight, like it had been for me. But in our eternities, it's only just a minute. But please hear me, this is why we need to trust and be obedient now — so we can have peace and freedom from this thing weighing us down and hurting us so very much.

Dear friend, I sit here today, many years into my desperate in-between, with a completely grateful heart, one I have chosen to use to trust God. I choose Him. I opt to let Him be the one to whom I turn for everything. I cannot imagine where I'd be if I didn't know Him and let Him carry me through these tremulous flames. If you haven't turned to Him to let Him carry you through, I'd like to take this opportunity to personally invite you to take the first step today. Take me by the hand. Let's do it together!

Chapter Eight

Waiting Room

Friend, time is a funny thing. If you're anything like me, you want what you want, and you want it on your schedule.

But what should we do when we think God isn't "on time?" What happens when He doesn't show up when we think He should? When we're wanting Him to make things right, right now, and He doesn't? We know He can. He knows it's what we want. But He just doesn't.

Martha and Mary—the same sisters who we previously visited—sent word to Jesus that their brother, Lazarus, was sick and requested Jesus come right away. Jesus and the disciples stayed where they were for two more days after learning the news, and then Jesus announced that Lazarus had died and they were finally going to him. By the time Jesus and the disciples arrived, Lazarus had been dead and in his tomb for four agonizing days.

Let's talk about the significance of four days before we move on. This is important because in Judaism, it's believed that after a person dies, the spirit hovers over the body, waiting to reenter, for three days. This is called *Shemira*. After the first three days, the appearance of the body changes, and the spirit departs for good. So Jesus was waiting until after Lazarus's spirit had surely left his body before arriving on the scene. This was certainly not Martha and Mary's timing.

When Martha heard Jesus was close, she went out to meet Him and told Him that if He'd been there, Lazarus would not have died. Then she confirmed her trust in God—saying she knew the Father would give Jesus whatever He asked for. (I'm pretty sure she's telling Jesus to bring Lazarus back from the dead.)

Jesus wept, as told in the shortest verse in the Bible (John 11:35). He then went to Lazarus's tomb, where He wept some more. After, Jesus demanded the stone be removed from the front of the tomb. Martha reminded Jesus how bad Lazarus would smell—you know, since he'd been dead for four days. "Stinketh" is the word in the KJV.

Jesus prayed to the Father: "Father, I thank you that you have heard me. I knew that you always hear me, but I said this for the benefit of the people standing here, that they may believe that you sent me" (John 11:41-42). Then Jesus called out in a loud voice, "Lazarus, come out!" (John 11:43). Lazarus, who had been dead for one day more than what the spirit would tolerate, walked out of the tomb with his hands and feet wrapped in strips of linen and a cloth around his face. Lazarus had been brought back to life—in God's timing (John 11:1-44).

God didn't show up when Martha or Mary wanted Him to. He didn't show up when it was convenient or easier. Or less painful. Or when it made the most sense to everyone else. It wasn't anyone's timing but God's—His divine and perfect timing.

In this story and probably in your story—and in mine—the timing was just as Jesus said: "This sickness will not end in death. No, it is for God's glory so that God's Son may be glorified through it" (John 11:4).

As Martha and Mary waited for Jesus to arrive, they fretted in their "waiting room." And this place that we're in, right at this moment, is our waiting room. This is our in-between space, where we heal and wait and grow and learn to be this new person God is putting us back together to be. This new version will be battle-tested, ready for Him, and He will use what we've been through for His glory. All the hurt and healing is to help others. To love and serve and give. This is the space between the burden and the blessing. This middle is God's space. A *kairos* moment. The moment God intervenes and enters our space. There is work to be done here. We are not alone, and we don't have to do the work alone, either.

Surrounded by Buckets of Testosterone

It was a beautiful summer morning in Flagstaff, Arizona. The air was cool, and the pine trees smelled amazing: fresh, with a crisp, clean, earthy, and uplifting fragrance. The birds sang their blessed songs, and I tried to let them settle my tummy. Amid the tall pines swaying gently in the cool breeze, adventure awaited. Well, an adventure for some. It'd be a day filled with tears, fear, anxiety, overcoming, and learning to take the next step—at least for me. I had the mantra, "Do it scared," on repeat in my mind.

I stood in a circle of abundant testosterone and excitement, trying not to let my nerves show through. Dylan, my youngest son, my brother-in-love (what I call my brother-in-law), and my nephew played and danced and launched playful banter back and forth. They were excited for what was to come and couldn't wait to get harnessed up. We signed all of the waivers to release the company from any burden of death and admit no liability. We got fitted for our harnesses and ropes and went through a few brief words of safety and caution. Basically, *if you fall, your rope will catch you, so you shouldn't die.*

The obstacle courses we were to be going through would include rope swings, hanging nets, ziplines, wobbly bridges, balance beams, and much more. And we mustn't forget the promise of other suspended "surprises." All would have various levels of elevation and difficulty. What the heck was I thinking?

I think I'll share, just in case you haven't caught on yet, I'm crazy afraid of heights. I also like to be in control of my own person. I've never been a fan of feeling afraid or fearing for my life. I don't seek opportunities for adrenaline rushes. If I do find myself in a prolonged adrenaline rush, I sleep for many hours after. But there I was, doing this thing that put me way out of my comfort zone. To be fair, I'd been living in fear and way out of my comfort zone for a long time at this point, and I must've just thought, "Why not go all in?" I seemed to be jumping off the deep end. And on purpose. With consent this time.

We began with a brief training course, which included various obstacles like those mentioned above. They were low to the ground and allowed you to feel more comfortable with everything before progressing to the more challenging, higher, scarier activities. Even in these beginning moments, I still felt like I was going to throw up. My breaths were shallow and uneven and full of fear. Crossing the first elevated and suspended sections successfully and planting my feet firmly on the next suspended, stable platform, my eyes filled with tears. I had done it! I'd made it. I didn't fall. I didn't die. I smiled, feeling proud of myself, as my gloved hands quickly wiped the tears from my cheeks before the boys could see.

Meanwhile, the four buckets of testosterone that accompanied me through this day were laughing and having the best time. Jumping and playing and swinging everything that would swing and bounce everything that would bounce to create more challenge for themselves—and probably others too. They pushed and teased each other; it was so much fun to watch. I quickly learned that I needed to let them go before me so that I could avoid any extra scary moments.

As I stood on a tall platform nailed to what looked like a telephone pole, preparing for the next task, tears streaked down my cheeks at a faster rate, and I took slow, deep breaths, trying to calm my nerves and tummy. With white knuckles, I took one step onto the next obstacle. And the next step. And the next. More deep breaths. More white knuckles. More tears. But I kept going despite the fear in my body and focused on the courage in my soul. I traversed tight ropes, climbing obstacles, and swinging ropes, where the ground disappeared beneath me.

I was in fight-or-flight mode the entire time.

So, so many years, months, and days had led up to that moment. I had to fight to find the will to keep going. To go one step at a time. To prove to myself that I could do it, that I was strong enough. Even though I felt like I was going to throw up at any moment, I chose to be brave.

In our crisis, I wondered then as I do now: How long do we keep holding on? How many more steps must we take?

I didn't make it through the entire course, but I did make it much farther than I ever thought I could. I was exhausted from the anxiety I'd been battling for hours, and I just didn't feel like I had the strength to finish without falling. And the idea of falling, even though I'd be caught by the rope, was enough to call the end.

But I had a pretty great view there, standing below the crazy guys, *my guys*, watching them swing through the treetops like monkeys, laughing, and living their best lives. I don't know if any of them had any fears going into the day, but from the place I was standing in those end-of-day moments, it sure didn't seem like it. I was so proud of them and the example they set of not letting fear get in the way of their fun. And for them, it was just that. Fun! I learned a lot from them that day.

I could have sat it out. I could have avoided going on the adventure in the trees and sat below for all of it, only to be a witness. I could have deemed myself a "cheerleader." But I didn't. I chose to stand up and take the risk. To be brave and show myself and others that I'm stronger and more capable than I thought. I got further than I thought I would by reaching each scary platform nailed to a tree, and through teary eyes and fighting to control my breath, I took one more step out onto that rope, onto that swing, or went for that giant leap.

> *It is in these hard, brave spaces where we find something good on the other side.*

It may be something big and life-changing. And it may be something small, like me getting way further on an adventure course in the tops of trees. The most important part is that we believe in it for ourselves. When we are in the middle of our hurts or hard things, it's pretty easy to stop believing that our lives will be anything other than the hard stuff we're going through. Sometimes, it's easy to believe it's always going to be a certain way. We're always going to hurt or be lonely or struggle. And we stop believing we can experience goodness or that we even deserve goodness. We must believe we can laugh and that it's okay when we do! *That we should.*

Alone in the Shadows

If our enemy can keep you isolated, he can keep you down. If he can keep you isolated, he can keep you questioning God's faithfulness. God's goodness. The truthfulness of His promises. If Satan can keep you isolated, he can control you. If he can keep you isolated, he can keep you miserable and broken. He can destroy you there in the loneliness. Any promise of safety in isolation is a lie he's telling you to keep you in a place where he can continue his attack. He will break you down, one solitary moment at a time.

In my prayer time, I felt God place a word on my heart: *community.*

I heard it whispered often.

I thought, *Well, I have community.* I had a couple of best friends who had been through it all with me. Dylan and my youngest son were there, and I had other family too. A few friends we did things with knew a little, so that felt kinda safe. I didn't think we needed to go deep with the rest. We had a group we gathered with, and I knew they would be there for us if we needed them. They didn't know anything detailed about us, but that was okay. I felt set. *All good here. Thanks!*

I continued my prayers for more healing. And more whispers and nudges came forth.

Community.

Community.

Community.

I recognized the frequency, and apparently, my appeal to God that I was all set, that I already had a great community around me, wasn't true. He wanted more for me.

I prayed, "Father, if you want me in community, then I trust You'll lead me to where I'm supposed to go. Show me."

God added more nudges to the prompting, and I found myself checking our church's app for a small women's Bible study group. Keyword: *small*.

Full. Full. Full. Evenings. Weekends. Too many women. Too early in the morning. *Nope, that won't work.* I saw no communities for me.

Some time passed, and I went back into the app. Right there was a group I'd never seen before. The meeting time was a little earlier in the morning than I wanted, but I could do it. I went to my first meeting, and it just so happened that it was the actual first meeting of the entire group. I was blessed with a one-on-one meet-up with the precious woman who'd answered the call to start the group. The next week, another precious sister came, and for a while, it was just the three of us. Thank you, Jesus, for *small*.

Occasionally, someone new would show up, and sometimes they'd stay with us, while sometimes, it wasn't a good fit. But God has grown our community group, and I feel so truly blessed. I've been in this community for years now, and I won't give the sisterhood up. I feel like God has hand-picked amazing women for me to do life with. We get to pour into one another, pray for each other, and support and hold each other accountable, and I am so grateful that God loves me enough to press me to look for the communities He is leading me to.

Now, just because I was in a new community, it didn't mean the enemy wasn't working to stop me from going. As I mentioned, it was kinda early morning for me to get up and be all ready and to the coffee shop on time. I was really feeling tired! When I started not sleeping well—often sleep didn't come at all—I grew even more tired and struggled to want to go. I told myself it was too much, that if I took a break, I'd sleep better the next week. That's when I stopped maneuvering, instantly, and realized what was happening: the enemy was winning. I committed right then and there that even if I didn't sleep at all, I was going to get up and go to that meeting and be surrounded by this wonderful community that I'd been led to! I could always take a nap later!

As you can tell, I love the ladies from my early morning Bible study, and as you can imagine, I felt quite content with this great community God had created. I was settled. I was learning to trust and slowly be more vulnerable and open. Over the years, I've learned to trust and not fear new interactions. I'm learning to be loved and to receive praise and acknowledgment. I'm learning the importance of being supported.

However, after joining, I still felt the prompting.

Community.

By that time, I was more open to saying, "Okay, Father. Show me the way."

Several months had passed and an acquaintance on Facebook shared an invite with me to a women's group. From what I could tell, it was a Christian women entrepreneur networking group, and I figured I'd check it out. The meeting date arrived, but something that needed my attention came up, and I just couldn't drop the thing and go. I vowed to go to the next meet-up.

The next one came, and something else "too important to miss" arrived, and again, I vowed to go *next* time. This happened again and again (like the flat tire). Finally, Dylan looked at me, with my hair done and makeup on, and asked if my meeting was that day. I explained that his dental emergency took precedence, that I'd skip it to take care of him. I'd just catch the next one. Thank God for good husbands because he told me I'd better grab my purse and get going because it sounded like Satan was succeeding in keeping me from that meeting—again! He was right. Satan had kept me from four meetings, and it was time to get going.

> If Satan was keeping me from that meeting, there must be a reason why I needed to be there.

Friend, I grabbed my purse and got in the car and went! If Satan was keeping me from that meeting, there must be a reason why I needed to be there.

And there was. I found the most precious women at that meeting.

I've only missed a couple of meet-ups since then. I was led to more than one community, where I learned to be vulnerable. Through them, I have now learned to trust. I have learned to lean on sisters in Christ. I'm still learning to let love in and be lifted up. I'm learning to lean on others in my times of need and struggle. I'm learning to take down the walls around my heart, one heavy brick at a time. I'm learning.

It is in community where healing comes. Praise comes. Beautiful smiles, hugs, and shared tears are our common connections. None of them share my specific pain, but together, we move toward healing from our individual trials. It is together that we can do this hard space in the middle.

> "Two are better than one; because they have a good reward for their labour. For if they fall, the one will lift up his fellow: but woe to him that is alone when he falleth; for he hath not another to help him up" (Ecclesiastes 4:9-10, KJV).

> "How good and pleasant it is when God's people live together in unity!" (Psalm 133:1).

> "And let us consider how to stir up one another to love and good works, not neglecting to meet together, as is the habit of some, but encouraging one another" (Hebrews 10:24-25, ESV).

Together We Rebuild

In Arizona during the summer months, when the heat stifles and the humidity rolls in, we get "Monsoon Season." For most of the year, you can hear us Arizonans saying, "It's a dry heat," and that's the truth. Dry heat as in open-an-oven-door, in-your-face dry heat. And, if you've ever been in hot and humid areas, dry heat is way more bearable. But in the hot of our summer, the humidity and dew points rise, and we become humid-hot. That's hot-hot. The blessing in the humidity hitting a certain point is that it brings in the monsoons—and the monsoon rains drop the temperatures. Then, for several weeks, we repeat that cycle many times.

During the Monsoon Season, you can see the dark clouds on the outskirts of town. It appears as if the mountains are holding them back, like a rope holding a fighter back. When the temperatures and dew points get to the perfect levels, the clouds leap over the mountains and make their way into town. Often, the storm system looks like a black wall advancing. It's beautiful and powerful and can sometimes be very scary. The storms come with intense winds and often cause a lot of destruction, including flash flooding and falling trees.

WAITING ROOM

Sometimes the monsoons produce a different kind of storm called a *haboob*. This isn't boob sweat, but we certainly have that too! A haboob is a giant dust storm that comes in, much like the monsoon rain storms, except this giant wall is brown and comprised of dirt and wind. The winds are still destructive, and when it's passed, everything is covered in dirt. No rain comes with them to clean off the earth. All you get is the mess.

In our stories, the actual chaos and initial pain of our storms may have settled, like the chaos and mess of the haboob, but the aftermath of destruction makes it impossible to return to any form of our previous normal. This is the reality of my current life. There is a new normal. I go to bed. I wake up. This is it. It's not bad. I know I am blessed right now. Life is just *different*.

I don't share this to drag you into my pain. I want you to know you are not alone. And you were never meant to do this alone. If you have been alone, please let this be a whisper to call you out. To call you into community. To call you into a community that can celebrate you and love you — and teach you to stand again and smile. And that it's okay to do so!

Memories still hurt. Tears still flow. Methods of healing still continue. Triggers happen, and I still need to process them. Not feeling yourself with the weight of the emptiness left behind means suffering can go on for what seems to be an unending string of days, months, and even years. God's promises (in His timing) are true, though you've begged Him, have yet to arrive, and are feeling disappointed. There are delays in your singing praises about His miracles for the entire world to hear.

We've been hurt, but we don't have to live hurt. All of your tears are, if you let them, your letting go of the hurt so you can receive possibility, laughter, and love. Maybe not the way you expected it, but remember: these tears and pain are not God's plan.

This tragedy can be your testimony that God is your rock, your solid foundation. Show the world that Satan picked the wrong girl! Satan can't hold you down!

> "Weeping may endure for a night, but joy cometh in the morning" (Psalm 30:5, KJV).

Big problems require God sized solutions. I've learned this. I've also experienced how "Blessed is the one who trusts in the Lord" (Psalms 40:4). God is not picking on me; He is picking *me*. He is choosing me to live out His blessings.

> "And everyone who calls on the name of the Lord will be saved. . . . There will be deliverance, as the Lord has said, even among the survivors whom the Lord calls" (Joel 2:32).

WAITING ROOM

As I sit in a comfy chair, with my legs tucked underneath me, across from a dear friend in the cozy living room of their cabin, she stops talking, looks me straight in the eyes, and says, "You must be pretty important if both God and the enemy are fighting for you." And I smile at the repetitive nature of God's goodness.

Sometimes in the hurt and the suffering, it's easy to think the world is out to get us. Or we can get caught up on all the things we've done wrong. But what if that's just the enemy trying to keep us down because he knows just how precious we are to our Father, and he's trying to keep us for himself.

Choose community. It's worth it.

Chapter Nine

Forgiving the Unforgivable

Friend, here we are, at the topic of forgiveness.

We've come so far, and as we've journeyed, I imagine you suspected this topic would be something we'd be diving into together. Forgiveness is a critical step in healing. If we want to be free from the weight of the past. Forgiveness is the only way to release the true burden. Forgiveness in no way erases the things you've endured or the pain people have caused. But it will free you from carrying the suffering with you.

> *"And Jesus said, Father, forgive them, for they know not what they do"* (Luke 23:34, ESV).

This verse holds a special place in my heart. This was Jesus's prayer as He hung on the cross, after having been betrayed and rejected, beaten, and tortured. After being mocked and spat on. He prayed this prayer to the Father on behalf of all who played a part in His torment. They were unlike Jesus. They were not free from sin. And still, Jesus pled with the Father on their behalf. And I can't help but think of you and me—and those who have hurt you and me. Jesus is pleading with the Father for all of us too.

When my heart is weary and I can't figure out why I've had to endure such pain and suffering, and when my exhaustion is so much that I just need a minute—or 720 of them—I am reminded of this beautiful prayer. "Forgive them Father, for they know not what they do." I, too, must forgive. Jesus made a way for me to be forgiven.

In the King James Version of the Bible, the word *forgive* is used ninety-five times. And when Peter asks Jesus how many times we should forgive, Jesus responds with "seventy times seven" (Matthew 18:22). That's 490 times! That's a lot. Jesus also tells us that we must forgive so that our Father in Heaven will forgive us. That's pretty powerful. But we are no strangers to this information if we've been a Christ-follower for any time. We know forgiveness is expected of us. We know forgiveness will be a part of our journey in this broken in-between. And we know we will have hurts and disappointments stemming from everyday life with people, all of which we must forgive. Some circumstances and events will be easier than others. But you and I know this is part of the journey. We just need to remember to work on it.

Friend, I'm not sharing anything new here. We know what we're called to do, but sometimes it's just hard to do. I see you. I feel it too. Sometimes it seems it's necessary for us to hold on to unforgiveness just a little longer because our hearts really hurt. What happened to us was awful. And we are justified in our hurt—in an earthly sense. If we were to let it go quickly, we wonder if we are somehow making light of the things that happened. Are we excusing the wrong that was done? Are we forgetting that it ever happened?

The answer is no. Forgiveness benefits us and does not equal forgetfulness.

Unforgiveness, on the other hand, is staying stuck in the past and in the pain. Unforgiveness is replaying old wounds over and over, allowing them to hurt us repeatedly, much like reopening a wound, never allowing it to scab and heal. Unforgiveness is deciding to let the pain and suffering fester. We hold on to it, guarding it like some prized possession, which will cause it to boil up and explode in ways we will regret. It will turn us into bitter and ugly people—people we don't want to be.

I don't want that for either of us, and I feel pretty confident in stating that God doesn't want that for us, either.

Forgiveness is not easy. Our hurts can be deeply rooted, and often, a part of us wants to hold on to those stories as if they'll help soothe our pain or justify the choices we made or the things we've done. Or will do. But it won't. Forgiveness is the only way out of our stuck. Please don't get stuck here in this deep, deep hole of unforgiveness.

Hurt people hurt people. It's a catchy slogan, but I'm here to remind you, through this difficult topic, that you are wonderful, precious, and loved. You get to choose to forgive or not. You choose how long you hold on to your hurts. Your brokenness. Your suffering. I am sharing my heart with you about how important this step is and hope it makes some impact. I'm asking you, friend, to choose *you*. Choose your healing. Choose your growing and your purpose. Choose your happiness and peace. Choose your smile, your laugh.

Please choose to forgive. Choose to forgive those in your story. Choose to forgive God. And, please, choose to forgive yourself.

One more reminder: don't stress about the timeline. Be patient with yourself on your forgiveness journey. Bring it to God continually. Ask Him to help you. It may take some time, but please keep moving forward, one faithful step at a time.

In his book, *Outliers*, Malcolm Gladwell said it takes ten thousand hours of deliberate practice to become an expert in any skill. Well, in life, we probably get ten thousand hours of opportunities to practice forgiveness to help us master this command. Practice in forgiving others can come to us through small daily occurrences, such as getting the wrong coffee order, someone cutting us off in traffic, or a stranger being rude at the grocery store. We can recognize these events throughout our day and use them to practice our forgiveness skills, intentionally looking for opportunities to practice forgiving others.

Seventy times seven, remember? The point is, it's going to take time and continual practice. So give yourself grace. Just keep working at it. Share each step of your healing with God so He can lead you on your journey. Keep moving forward and practicing.

And, of course, there will be the "big" things that will require more work. We may experience different forms of betrayal — a loved one saying hurtful words to us; physical, emotional, or verbal abuse; stolen property; unkept promises; the list goes on. These hurts will take more time, more help from God, and more effort than our small daily practices. But when we recognize and work on the small ones, these larger ones will be a little easier to tackle when they come.

When we find ourselves in a place where we have bigger offenses to forgive, we should first take our hurts to our Heavenly Father in prayer. We can ask Him to guide and direct our paths toward forgiveness, especially if we're not feeling ready. He alone can change our hearts. We should ask Him to show us areas where we still have personal work to do: the what, who, and where we still need to forgive. We must do the work. Journaling, EFT tapping especially using scripture as our truth statements, and other healing modalities are amazing. If you need further help or direction, seek counseling or coaching. Just don't get stuck in the cycle. Forgiveness is a "through-it activity." We have to move through it.

Unstuck Yourself

A word of caution here as we work on healing and forgiveness. We can easily get stuck in this forgiveness cycle. We aren't supposed to get stuck inside the process, like it's some big washing machine, thinking we need to forgive the same offense over and over again. That's not how this works. If that's happening to you, the enemy is keeping you stuck. We are to forgive and move forward. There is no need to forgive the same thing more than once. Releasing is part of the forgiveness process. It's about releasing the hurts and those involved to God and releasing ourselves from carrying the weight of it all. Know that God's got you. Lay it all at His feet and do not pick it back up.

Learning Self-Forgiveness

If you're stuck in the forgiveness place of self-condemnation, where you're working through the same event, it might be time to ask God to show you who *you are* in His eyes. Maybe it's time to allow Him to make you a new creation. Friend, maybe it's time to forgive yourself. Yes, it is necessary to forgive yourself for the role you played in your hurt. Maybe you didn't respond the way you wanted to, and you need to forgive yourself for that. Maybe you hurt someone you love, and you've received their forgiveness, but you haven't forgiven yourself? Maybe you made a decision you regret, and God has already forgiven you, but you can't seem to let go of the guilt and shame you've placed on yourself. Or maybe you need to forgive yourself for picking up that same hurt over and over again and not letting it go.

I remember the moment I understood that I was in this place of unforgiveness. I realized I needed to forgive myself. I was focused on forgiving everyone else, so I really wanted to heal in this area, and I asked God to show me where I needed to forgive. That's when I learned forgiveness of self.

When I realized what I was doing to myself, it felt like a ton of bricks had hit me. I did a lot of prayerful journaling around this idea and allowed the Holy Spirit to guide me in the list of things I needed to forgive myself for. A couple of the things I learned was 1) not being able to rescue my children from being alienated from me—I couldn't protect them or make it stop, and I still can't, and 2) I needed to forgive myself for not knowing the warning signs of alienation and seeing what was happening to them. It was eye-opening to learn I had been carrying around so much unforgiveness for myself. I was proud of how far I had come in my forgiveness journey, but I had left out a very important person: me!

It was in this season that I learned to love myself as God loves me. I was carrying around so much unforgiveness and shame for all that I had been through that I not only wasn't forgiving myself, but I also wasn't loving myself. I learned long ago not to speak negatively about myself. But in this season, I learned that ignoring myself was just as bad as speaking negatively toward myself because ignoring—that is neglect. Neglect is just as abusive as verbal abuse. So please, friend, forgive yourself. Take the time to follow the process and heal all the things you need to forgive yourself for.

I used journaling and self-reflective activities to process emotions. After I learned the healing exercise I describe in the next section, it became a wonderful resource on my self-forgiveness journey.

> Always let the Holy Spirit guide you to confirm that the healing modalities are aligned with God's Word.

Be prayerful as you do any healing activities, even with a counselor or coach. Ask that Jesus be present with you so you can feel His love. Always let the Holy Spirit guide you to confirm that the healing modalities are aligned with God's Word.

These healing activities may guide us in the steps, but our faithful Father in Heaven, who knows us and loves us, will direct us if there's anything specific we need in our healing practice.

Healing in Action

I was doing a forgiveness activity from a devotion written by Lysa TerKeurst called *The Forgiveness Journal*. It follows her book, *Forgiving What You Can't Forget*. You can take a moment to add them both to your Amazon cart. These resources have been helpful in my healing journey, and I believe they'll help you too.

In *The Forgiveness Journal* exercise, Lysa instructs readers to pick one person per forgiveness session. Then, we should repeat the steps at another time for someone different. She directs us to write one thing on separate note cards for each of the pains, feelings, events, unmet expectations, etc., which we would be forgiving this person for.

I said a prayer, asking Jesus to be with me and for His Spirit to show me what and who I still needed to forgive. Someone came to mind. This wasn't my first time working through forgiveness for this person. New events were happening that needed new forgiveness. And I learned that some old hurts still needed some additional work.

I tearfully wrote out my items of forgiveness, each one on an individual card. Some items came quickly, while others seemed Holy Spirit-guided. I asked, "Okay, what else?" When I felt I was finished writing, I stacked the notecards into a neat pile. Per the instructions, I grabbed a stack of larger cards from my desk drawer to cover the smaller cards I had written on. The instructions said to use red cards or cloth for the exercise, but I didn't have these items, and I didn't want to wait for an Amazon delivery. I was feeling moved to take this step and do the activity right then. I have red cards now.

I sat on the floor with crossed legs, a box of tissues, and both stacks of cards in my lap. I took a few deep breaths and said a prayer. I spread the cards I'd written out on the floor in front of me and proceeded with the rest of the exercise. With each card, I said the person's name, followed by, "I forgive you for . . ." [then I read what I had written on the card]. There's something powerful in saying all of that out loud. With some of the cards, it seemed easy and gave me hope that this exercise would be a breeze. But then I got to some tough cards. The hurts that hurt the worst. Those that had pained me deep in my core. The events that were as bad as the moments they had originally taken place—the new and raw ones especially.

I knew I wasn't alone during this. I knew God saw my pain. I knew He saw my desire to be obedient and my longing to forgive and release the weight I'd been carrying around for so long. And I know He was healing me . . . and my unforgiveness.

Then I laid a larger card over the top of the card I had just read and said, "And whatever my feelings will not yet allow for right now, the blood of Jesus will surely cover it."

One by one, I worked my way through that pile of handwritten cards. Some were so painful that it took me a moment to speak the words out loud. They became stuck in my throat. The tears choked me, and all I could do was sit and feel the weight of all the pain I'd been carrying. I knew those would need divine intervention. It was at this time, on my office floor, with a puddle of tears on the floor between my folded legs, that I truly unlocked the deep freedom of forgiveness. I truly felt the weight lift from my tense and burdened shoulders.

I am no stranger to forgiveness. This moment was certainly not my first go at it. Throughout my life, I have had ample opportunities to forgive others. Up to this moment, I had forgiven plenty. And I felt pretty proud of myself for what a good forgiver I was. I believe one of my gifts is that I love deeply and forgive easily. Nonetheless, I learned I still had work to do.

When I had worked through most of the cards and only had three written cards left uncovered on the floor, I noticed I had exactly three larger cards left in my hand to cover them. There were three of each—and I had not counted out either pile before the exercise. I had just grabbed a handful of each of the cards from my desk drawer. To me, this felt like confirmation. A rush of love came over me. Tears of pure joy and gratitude welled up in my eyes. I stopped right then, mid-activity, and prayed, thanking God for this beautiful message. Another *kairos* moment. I believe, in God's perfect alignment, that He showed me He was there in that place! There, beside me all along, helping me process all of the pain, all of the tears, all of my brokenness and sorrow and grief and unforgiveness. He was with me, and the blood of Jesus was surely covering it all, including the parts I was still having a hard time forgiving.

> "Grief, I've learned, is really just love. It's all the love you want to give but cannot. All of the unspent love gathers in the corners of your eyes, in the lump in your throat, and in the hollow part of your chest. Grief is just love with no place to go." —Jaimie Anderson"

This next bit is not part of the original exercise, but remember, I suggested you pray and ask Jesus to be present, to let the Holy Spirit guide your personal healing journey. This is crucial because none of us is the same. No two of us have experienced the exact same events, and we don't process our pain the same way. We won't heal the same, either. Be prayerful on your journey so you can receive specific guidance on what you need.

I felt prompted to shred the written-out cards in the nearby paper shredder. One by one, I declared, "I forgive you, [name]," as I fed each card individually through the paper shredder. Just before I began shredding, I counted the cards. There were twenty-four small cards. I looked up the biblical meaning of twenty-four and learned it represents God's power and authority. I was feeling His power and authority over this forgiveness activity!

The following day at church, the pastor said that Satan was called by twenty-four different names in the Bible. In that healing and forgiveness activity the day before, God prompted me to write about twenty-four pains I had been carrying, things I needed to forgive and let go. And He had me pull twenty-four cards to cover Satan's plan of pain, suffering, and destruction with the blood of Jesus. God's power and authority were over this activity. And He showed up in the exact number of ways Satan had.

"For we do not wrestle against flesh and blood, but against the rulers, against the authorities, against the cosmic powers over this present darkness, against the spiritual forces of evil in the heavenly places" (Ephesians 6:12, ESV).

> "Be sober-minded; be watchful. Your adversary the devil prowls around like a roaring lion, seeking someone to devour" (1 Peter 5:8, ESV).

But God. He is always there for us!

Embracing Healthy Boundaries

Friend, forgiveness does not mean that we should or are required to become vulnerable again to the person who hurt us.

I needed to hear this message on my healing journey. So let's repeat it: *Forgiveness does not mean we should or are required to become vulnerable again to that person who hurt us.* Period. This is a personal boundary and a decision you must prayerfully make for yourself. There are times when forgiveness can be met with a continued relationship, maybe with specific boundaries in place. But in other cases, it won't be safe to go into a relationship with the person who hurt us again. Only you and God can make this decision. Forgiveness does not mean the events never took place. It just means you're not allowing those hurts to continue to hurt you, hold you back, or anchor you in the past any longer.

Often, forgiveness does not come with an apology. It doesn't come with a return or do-over for what took place. It often doesn't even come with an acknowledgment that the event even happened at all. Sometimes, forgiveness doesn't involve the other person, ever. It really has nothing to do with them—besides releasing yourself from the heavy load of carrying them and the heartbreak they've caused you with you every day.

God...Why?

When we are in painful places that break us to dust, we wonder why God allowed these horrible things to happen. Sometimes we may question His goodness or love. Some wonder if He was so good, why can't everything in life just be good too?

Just because we are believers and we have a great relationship with Jesus, it doesn't keep us from suffering. It doesn't make us exempt from going through some really tough things in this garden between gardens. Maybe even lots of things. We will feel the hurts of this broken world; no one gets off scot-free, not even Jesus. And all of this may cause some feelings of anger and frustration toward God.

If this is you, and you're in a place where you are angry with God, where you are mad at Him for "allowing" these horrible things to happen to you—if you see yourself in this place and these hurt feelings are causing you to distance yourself from Him or question if you even want to have a relationship with Him—know this: Your feelings matter to God. He loves you. He is strong and can handle your hurt. He will have compassion on you, regardless of your feelings or your anger. Go to Him. Go sit with Him and share with Him all the feelings you have toward Him. Ask Him all of your unanswered questions. He knows your suffering, and He desperately wants you to come to Him. He can handle it. God wants to love you through this. He wants to walk you through these harbored feelings. Don't hide. Don't distance yourself. Run to Him, not away from Him.

Some people wonder how to do this. Well, you can write letters to God. You can sit in silence with Him or ask Him to show Himself to you. Ask Him to show you all the good He plans to bring out of all of this brokenness. Scream. Cry. Whatever you must do, just do it with Him. In doing so, He will bring you peace as you trust Him.

> "Put on the whole armor of God, that you may be able to stand against the schemes of the devil. For we do not wrestle against flesh and blood, but against the rulers, against the authorities, against the cosmic powers over this present darkness, against the spiritual forces of evil in the heavenly places. Therefore take up the whole armor of God, that you may be able to withstand in the evil day, and having done all,

> to stand firm. Stand therefore, having fastened on the belt of truth, and having put on the breastplate of righteousness, and, as shoes for your feet, having put on the readiness given by the gospel of peace" (Ephesians 6:11-15, ESV).

Forgive God for yourself. Remember, you are the benefactor of forgiveness. And if you need help with this because your hurt is too heavy, take that to Him too. Ask Him to help you. He will.

Chapter Ten

Beyond the Rearview

God was calling me to something, and I had, for quite some time, let the enemy hold me back. Satan had convinced me that if I listened to God and did this thing — writing this book — that He asked me to do, I would have continual persecution, judgment, and more attacks. And after all I'd been through in the past too many years, this scared me beyond measure. I didn't feel strong enough to endure reliving all of my pain and any possible new pain.

In addition to those initial lies, the enemy told me I wasn't good enough — that I didn't have the skills or knowledge and that nobody would want to hear what I had to say. These promises of the enemy — anti-promises — pushed me into a state of fear and insecurity about moving forward in the calling God had laid on my heart. He reminded me that I've been writing since I was a small child, and this was His gift. He then brought me the additional training I'd been asking Him for and poured into me who He says I am. God's promises are so much greater than Satan's lies!

I read a quote — I don't remember when, and I can't seem to find the author now — that greatly impacted me, so I wrote it down. "When I'm not courageous, it's not a sign that I'm a coward so much as an indication that I'm failing to embrace love."

This insight hit me right in the gut like a full-force back-kick from Jackie Chan. That my being disobedient (or slow) to the calling I was so strongly feeling was me not receiving the love God was giving me.

He was calling me to be courageous in what He was asking me to do. And also to receive His love and whatever blessings He had in store for me within and on the other side of my obedience. Wow! Just wow! I know He was with me through it all. I knew He would make a way where there was no way. I knew He would give me the strength to endure. I am so grateful for this message—and grateful that God is always faithful.

He is constantly coming after me. Seeking me. Growing me. Loving me. And I know He's coming after you as well!

> "And the God of all grace, who called you to his eternal glory in Christ, after you have suffered a little while, will himself restore you and make you strong, firm and steadfast"
> (1 Peter 5:10).

He promises us that after we have suffered a little while, He Himself will restore us and make us strong! Oh, can I get a hallelujah?!

This is sooo good! This is the promise we can stand firm in. This is where all the suffering changes. We will be restored: strong, firm, and steadfast! And He promises that He Himself will be the one to do it!

We have been given new hope for restoration. Even in the restoration that looks different from what we thought it would. Jesus rose from the grave. I'm sure that restoration looked very different from what those around Him thought it would. Through Christ, God's promise to make everything new has been validated in Jesus's resurrection.

> "He will wipe every tear from their eyes. There will be no more death or mourning or crying or pain, for the old order of things has passed away. He who was seated on the throne said, 'I am making everything new!'"
> (Revelation 21:4-5).

Women at the Well

I was at a women's conference with several people I had met in my new women's group. I hadn't had much opportunity to get to know them or be vulnerable enough to share much of my story since we'd only known each other for a couple of months. This three-day conference had me sobbing almost the entire time. God was moving me into a space of vulnerability, and I believe He was using these smaller opportunities to show me I was safe as He prepared me for the bigger vulnerability He had called me to in writing this book. He was asking me to share pieces of my story and my heartbreak to lift and love others who desperately need to know they are not alone. Those searching for hope needing to learn they're worthy of love! Though the enemy told me that every time I opened my mouth and shared any of the deepest, darkest parts of my soul, I would be attacked, the truth was I wasn't. I was loved.

During this conference and the Holy Spirit-inspired sobbing I had no control over, there was a moment when I was so taken over by the emotions that I squatted down in front of my chair to hold myself steady and give myself a small space of privacy. I just needed a minute. The Holy Spirit was so strong, and God's love was heavy in that room filled with other women who were all going through their own things.

As I knelt in front of my chair, I felt a woman come over the backside of my chair and wrap her arms around me to just hold me. After a few moments, she whispered in my ear through her own tears and pain that she was so terribly broken. That she had given up her children, left them, and felt so heartbroken by what she had done. She sobbed through my hair. She held onto me for a long time, with my one arm reaching up and wrapped around her shoulder.

After the session ended, my new friends and I made our way from our seats and out of the auditorium to get some fresh air, a woman—I believe the same one—ran down the aisle with a single rose in her hand and handed it to me, tears streaming down her tear-stained cheeks. I can't remember if she said anything, but I know she was giving me a gift of beauty and love. And she gave me the gift of her vulnerability. She had shared with me the brokenness she was feeling. She shared with me something she possibly hadn't shared with anyone else. This stranger showed me the way. Brave and firm on the foundation of the One who loves her unconditionally, she had answered a nudge. She moved where God told her to move. She did what she felt she was being called to do. And it served me right where I needed it. There were hundreds of women in that room. But God led her to me.

This woman had no idea that I'd lost my children. Yet, there she was, confessing to me that she had given hers up. She had no idea that my pain was similar but opposite. Her heart was breaking her, and, in her brokenness, she was wrapping her love around me. In her vulnerability, she was teaching me that instead of the lies of the enemy promising me persecution and judgment by all, I would be loved.

Later, when the evening wrapped up, we left the auditorium in a slow cluster, which allowed me to take a few deep breaths and shake out the emotion that had blanketed me for the majority of the day. Before everyone left, this small group of new friends and I took a few minutes to talk before going home to our waiting families. With swollen eyes and additional tears shed, I shared a tiny bit of what God was calling me to do. I shared with them the struggles of vulnerability and the wrestle I was having with God. I shared that every time I felt Him calling me out of the darkness to be brave, I met Him in my prayer closet with my objections and concerns. And every time I had a concern, He had a solution. One sweet sister looked at me with complete love and said, "This is vulnerability in community, for God's glory." And she was completely right!

He was calling me to small victories of vulnerability. Since then, He keeps prompting me with much larger tasks. None of this has happened overnight. It's all been one small step at a time. And I still made several visits to my prayer closet with objections in mind, but those were followed by His faithfulness to get me to where He wanted me to go. A prompting from the Holy Spirit. An obedient step with a deep breath and a little more bravery than I had the time before. And the cycle repeated until I was fully obedient. Fully committed to the journey He was leading me on.

And this, my friend, is why you and I are here together right now. God has met my every concern, every objection, every fear, and every negative belief, so I can't ignore what He has called me to do. He's met me with love—at events, with promptings, with strangers, and with a sisterhood of community where He taught me that Satan is a liar. I am safe even if the judgment and persecution come because I believe Jesus was telling the truth when He said we would be mocked and persecuted as God's people and that others would lie and say all sorts of evil things against us. Even then, we are His! We are safe in Him (Matthew 5:11).

God has led me to do all of this with wonderful women who speak truth in love with me. And now, I'm here to do that for you! You deserve love and truth. You deserve purpose. You deserve God's promise of becoming new.

It is time for us to stand up and step out wearing our "Not Today Satan" T-shirts and let Him lead us into the small moments where He can prove to us that Satan is a liar. And that we are, in fact, brave. That we are chosen. And loved. And enough. That all the lies Satan is feeding us to keep us broken are also keeping us from thriving, keeping us from helping and loving others, and keeping our lights hidden under the table. The enemy is holding us down and holding us back because he knows God's calling us to do important work. That work begins with us getting unstuck!

> "Neither do people light a lamp and put it under a bowl. Instead they put it on its stand, and it gives light to everyone in the house" (Matthew 5:15).

Let us step boldly out of the darkness and into God's calling.

> "You intended to harm me, but God intended it for good to accomplish what is now being done, the saving of many lives" (Genesis 50:20).

From *Darkroom* to Masterpiece

Many years ago, before digital cameras and cell phones, if you wanted to take photos, you had to buy a roll of film, load it into your camera—carefully, without exposing it and ruining the film—and then you could take your photos. Maybe you're old enough to remember the days when you had a roll of film for so long that you forgot what was on the film. Then, if you were like me, you'd drop the rolls of film off in an envelope (at Costco!), wait a few hours or days, and then go back and pick up your pictures, hoping some actually turned out. It felt like Christmas as you flipped through them to see what you got.

I never developed my own film even though I always thought it would be fun. When developing film, you had to be in a completely unlit room called a *darkroom*. In total darkness, you carefully removed the film from the canister, secured it in the reel, and then soaked the film in a couple of different solutions, including developer, stop bath, and fixer.

In the developer stage, the film was regularly agitated to ensure even development of the film and to dislodge any air bubbles that might attach themselves. Next, the film was put into the stopping solution to stop the process of development. Timing was pretty exact to ensure the film wasn't under or overdeveloped. After this, the fixer was applied, and more agitation was implemented. This is what set the image and made it no longer light-sensitive. When these stages were completed, the film was washed in running water and hung to dry.

So, for the film to be developed, the process was 1) remove it from its canister, 2) submerge it into the developer, 3) agitate it regularly, then 4) stop, fix it, rinse it off, and hang it. Do you see the pattern here?

In our hurting, in our dark places, we are removed from what we thought life would be like, or our canisters. It is in this darkroom (i.e., storm, pit, flames, etc.) where God develops us. We are soaked in the first solution and regularly agitated to ensure proper development, spiritually, emotionally, and physically. It is in these dark places where we are isolated and alone that He can implement His plan.

He stops us, for healing and then fixing. Eventually, God rinses us off and sets us out to shine our light, which is really His light—if we call ourselves Christians. We become vulnerable and share our stories. And love on others.

Just as the film turns into beautiful photographs, we become new creations. Beautiful masterpieces. He does a new thing in us.

Remember Lot's Wife

Back in Genesis 19 is the story of Lot. Two angels appeared to him to convince him to leave Sodom and Gomorrah so he wouldn't be destroyed with the wickedness that had overtaken the land. Lot and his family were told in verse 17 to "Flee for your lives! Don't look back and don't stop anywhere in the plain!" The Lord then rained down burning sulfur on Sodom and Gomorrah from the heavens, destroying all living things in the land. As Lot and his family fled, and against what Lot and his wife had been told, "Lot's wife looked back, and she became a pillar of salt."

It's believed that she looked back to see, one last time, all that she was leaving behind. And that act of disobedience, paired with a lack of devotion to the Lord, destroyed her. So we learn that Jesus said, "Remember Lot's wife" (Luke 17:32) to avoid looking back ourselves.

The Bible mentions about 170 women, but Jesus only talks about one—Lot's wife. This must be a pretty important message for Him to bring her up. Jesus tells us to remember Lot's wife because we are not supposed to be stuck in old, often sinful, places. We are not supposed to be looking back at what was left behind. We are being called ahead! We are only meant to be passing through all of this on our way to Glory.

Friend, if it was important enough for Jesus to remind us to remember Lot's wife not to look back, it must be pretty important in our journeys also. Yes, a lot has changed for us in our brokenness. Maybe even everything. Life. Family. Finances. And more. But we can't stop. We can't get stuck here. And most certainly, we can't go back. There's nothing there for us. So don't even look.

Unfortunately, that's easier said than done, right? That's exactly where we can so easily find ourselves. Maybe even right now. But that's where the enemy wants us—stuck in the past, wishing for old lives, instead of living in the blessings that God has given us in the *now*. We may not be enjoying the people and the children and family that remain with us. We may not be fully receiving the love of those around us because we are stuck in our old expectations. In the pain. In the shame. In the guilt. In the what "should have been." And in what was "supposed to be." Stuck longing for the love of those who are no longer with us in this chapter of life.

It is in this stuck place that we have prioritized the past over the present.

This is where we must learn that the priorities of the present and the future must outweigh those of the past. Jesus is with us in the now, right here in the present, and He is ready to take us into our future. He is ready to lead the way.

The new creation has come. The old has gone, and the new is here! Let us decide to walk in God's blessings, decide to walk in His healing. Let us decide to let Him lead the way and call us into the bigger picture that He has planned for us. So much more than the sorrows of the past.

This life of ours is not a story of our hurts, our pains, and our suffering. They were a part of the story, but they are not *the* story. This is the story of healing and hope and living out our divine purpose. You will share a unique hope for all when you're vulnerable enough to share your story because you know exactly what it feels like to be them.

> "Consider it pure joy, my brothers and sisters, whenever you face trials of many kinds, because you know that the testing of your faith produces perseverance. Let perseverance finish its work so that you may be mature and complete, not lacking anything. If any of you lacks

> wisdom, you should ask God, who gives generously to all without finding fault, and it will be given to you. But when you ask, you must believe and not doubt, because the one who doubts is like a wave of the sea, blown and tossed by the wind." (James 1:2-6).

Straighten Your Crown

The Bible refers to the crown of life as a gift from God that will be awarded to those who, because of their love for Him, faithfully endured trials and tests on earth. As James 1:12 tells us, "Blessed is the one who perseveres under trial because, having stood the test, that person will receive the crown of life that the Lord has promised to those who love him."

The crown of life isn't an actual crown but a symbolic representation of God's recognition for having triumphed in this life. This crown is God's reward for those who love Him and loyally persevere under trial. James wasn't the only one preaching on this. Jesus shares with us in the Sermon on the Mount: "Blessed are those who are persecuted because of righteousness, for theirs is the kingdom of heaven. Blessed are you when people insult you, persecute you and falsely say all kinds of evil against you because of me. Rejoice and be glad, because great is your reward in heaven" (Matthew 5:10-12).

On a particularly hard day, I sat at my desk, trying to get some work done. I just couldn't focus on the long list of tasks before me, so I paused. I let my head drop forward, with my chin to my chest, and just sat. No prayers came. I was all out of words. After a few silent moments, taking deep breaths, and basking in the quiet moment that I surely needed, I heard God's message that He wanted to share with me, to bring comfort to my weary soul. He said to my spirit, "Straighten your crown, beloved daughter. You are beautiful and strong and loved. Stand firm. I've got you." I immediately wrote this beautiful message down and taped it to my computer monitor. And that is where this beautiful gift will stay — right in front of me, to continually remind me of His love. I'm sharing this with you because I want this to be your reminder that God sees you too! When the moment is hard and you don't know what to say, let this be your reminder that you are loved and chosen!

It's Your Turn

Take out a sticky note and write it down — "Straighten your crown, beloved daughter. You are beautiful and strong and loved. Stand firm. I've got you" or something similar. Then put it where it can remind you of how much you're loved. Even on days you don't particularly feel it, take a deep breath, smile, straighten your crown, and read this love note from God out loud. And feel it!!!

> *"Straighten your crown beloved daughter. You are beautiful and strong and loved. Stand firm. I've got you." —God*

No matter what hardships, pain, and suffering you've endured, you can find comfort in knowing that God has huge blessings in store for you. Even if it comes as a simple, beautiful word He whispers to you in a quiet moment. Hold this close to your heart. He will use your story for His glory!

Declare in Jesus's Name

When Jesus was in the wilderness, fasting for forty days. Satan tempted Him several times. Jesus speaks God's truth over Himself. And we can too! I think it's time we stand up and, with a firm voice, speak as Jesus spoke: "Get behind me, Satan!" and "It is written: 'Worship the Lord your God and serve him only'" (Matthew 16:23 and Luke 4:8). We can and should take Jesus's lead and boldly speak God's truth over ourselves, our lives, and those we love.

Speaking God's truth over ourselves and our loved ones is simply declaring His Word as our truth, just as Jesus did. The world may call these positive affirmations, but that's because the world lives in, through, and for self. We live with the Holy Spirit. That was the gift Jesus left us. We are who God says we are, and one of the best things I've learned on this journey is to speak His truth over me—for truth, protection, and blessing.

> *"The tongue has the power of life and death"* (Proverbs 18:21).

This verse suggests we should choose to speak life with our words. Let us not use our words to hold us back or tear us down. Let's choose this moment to stop speaking brokenness and pain and suffering over ourselves. All of that is part of the story of the past. It's time we leave them there. It's time we receive His healing, blessings, and love. Speak them into your heart right now.

> *"'Have faith in God,' Jesus answered. Truly I tell you, if anyone says to this mountain, 'Go, throw yourself into the sea,' and does not doubt in their heart but believes that what they say will happen, it will be done for them"* (Mark 11:22-23).

I love this verse! I've seen miracles like this with my own eyes. Not long ago, we were in a particularly challenging time in life.

Just before sunrise on a June morning, our home had been robbed. Worldly possessions that had been collected over decades were loaded up into our SUV and left with the three masked and gloved men who broke into our home. Our identities and debit and credit cards had been stolen and used almost immediately. The hard place got harder and harder, and we felt the mountains of being violated and the loss closing in on us.

Still swirling in all of this chaos, we were then prompted to sell what remained, including our home, our RV, and our other vehicles. There was nothing more we could do in this situation besides have faith and hope and wait. Faithfully, we waited on God's timing and His will.

One Sunday, we sat in church, and the pastor's message was on this very verse in Mark 11. Our hearts were heavy in the midst of so much loss and letting go. Dylan squeezed my hand. Of course, tears ran down my face. This wasn't a one-tissue church service. The pastor yelled out, "Mountains be moved!" and called on us to repeat after him. One thing about me and the tears at church is that I can control them pretty well unless any words pass through my lips. So, when I'm feeling moved emotionally more than normal, I sometimes hold back, only lip-syncing the words to worship songs. On this day, feeling the squeeze of our current mountains and the call from pastor to repeat after him, I pulled a "Milli Vanilli." The pastor called for a louder repeat, "MOUNTAINS BE MOVED!" and a woman popped up out of her seat. With all of her vigor, all of her heart, and maybe some pain and love alongside her belief, she praised God. At the top of her lungs, she called out, "MOUNTAINS BE MOVED!!!" Oh, how I loved that woman! I loved her courage. I loved her faith. I loved that her voice broke through and spoke truth for me. With a laugh, my floodgates opened. "Mountains be moved!!!" I finally shouted.

Shortly after that Sunday, God faithfully moved every single mountain for us. And it all happened in a short period. There was no way to deny that it was Him. With everything that had unfolded, He made a way when, within our strength and might, there had been no way. And I should also give a reminder right here about something we already addressed: The moving of those particular mountains was in *His timing*.

I still have mountains He's not moved yet. Still, I know He is good. I know He loves me. I know His way is better than mine. I will remain faithful. *Thy will be done, oh Lord.*

"Let everything you say be good and helpful, so that your words will be an encouragement to those who hear them (including yourself)!" (Ephesians 4:29, NLT, addition in parentheses mine).

"Rejoice in the Lord always. I say it again: Rejoice!" (Philippians 4:4).

My friend, now is the time to joyfully praise our Father for being with us this entire time, for never leaving us alone in our darkest hours. For developing us in the darkness. For calling us to vulnerability and love. It is time we get unstuck and speak His words of truth over ourselves and those we love. It's time to declare all the blessings He has lined up for us and is ready for us to receive. He has something new and wonderful for us, and it's time for us to take the next step in faith and confidence! It's time to move mountains and give Him praise!

Chapter Eleven

Harvesting Joy

Friend, let's take a big deep breath, take our bras off, and settle into some comfy clothes. Let's pour ourselves fresh glasses of our favorite beverages and gear up to . . . keep on going. Because it's not over yet.

Just when we think we've found a smooth path, when we think we have done enough healing work and feel grateful for a minute to rest and fill our lungs with air, things are going to happen to disrupt us on our journeys.

When we get our smiles back, when we feel our steps are a little lighter and our shoulders a bit less tense — when we feel safe in the calm — we are inevitably going to get knocked off-balance. It just happens. I think it's called *life*.

Something is going to trigger a hurt that we didn't know was there. It's going to sting, maybe make us cry. Or it might make us want to scream and rant and rage — and that's okay. (I prefer screaming in my car, parked at the back of a parking lot so I don't scare anyone.) It's going to make us take the question *Why is this happening?* to our prayer closets once again.

And I'll be the one to say it: Friend, it is *our responsibility* to take the time and work on our healing some more. We will have little triggers (and maybe some gigantic ones) that come up to steal the breath from our lungs. There will be times when our guts feel like we are going to lose our lunches and put wobbles in our steps. It's going to happen.

Like in hockey and football, the players know the hit is coming. I don't believe we should expect it, necessarily, but knowing it's a possibility may make the blow a little less painful. If we anticipate that life isn't going to always be roses and champagne, and sometimes we'll bite into something gross (you know, that disgusting soft grape after you've had so many yummy crisp ones), we might process the trigger a little easier.

I enjoy taking an hour to myself, grabbing a coffee, and walking around a big superstore. I love all things "home," especially home décor and baking, so I usually spend most of my time walking up and down those aisles. It makes my heart so happy. Looking at new trends, squishing pillows to see if they're firm or soft. Touching all the fabrics and admiring the trendy colors and so many shiny things. Plus, I get in bonus steps.

On one of these beloved afternoons of peaceful department store aisle walking, while sipping my fresh cup of coffee, enjoying the tranquility of my happy place, and minding my own business, I turned the corner and came face-to-face with the baby section. It was filled with adorable clothing, blankets, accessories—all the baby things. Everything was so tiny and so darling. Immediately, my heart felt like a knife had pierced it. I was crushed. I stopped breathing, and enormous tears filled my eyes and then flowed down my previously happy cheeks. In an instant, my joyful heart was shattering all over again. I had no idea that this particular section of the store would trigger me in such a way. But it most definitely did. At this moment, it hit me that my daughter and I were missing out on so much by not being part of my new granddaughter's life. That little girl was missing out too! I desperately wanted to be involved, and my body decided to let me know I still had work to do to heal this new piece to my story.

I had already cried and journaled. I had brought my sorrow and my pain to God. I had shared with Him my unmet expectations. I'd given Him so many of my alligator tears. I had worked on releasing the expectations of what I thought life would be like at this stage in my life and the grieving of my world not looking at all like I thought it would.

But in that aisle, carrying remnants of all of my previous expectations, I realized I had not fully processed everything. All of it just got to me, and I came apart one thread at a time—but very quickly. I couldn't have planned for it. I hadn't expected it. It just happened.

Not to be a downer here, but sweet friend, these hard moments are going to happen for you too. I think that's a part of love, certainly of healing. It's a process that goes up and down, not straight up. I don't know what your triggers are going to look like. I don't know what moments will make you stumble or where you'll be when the time comes, but I know there will be setbacks. There will be painful memories that erupt from triggering moments. We're going to feel the hurt.

> I believe these trigger moments tell us where we still have work to do.

But guess what? We can view these as blessings. I believe these trigger moments tell us where we still have work to do. Where we still have hurts we must give over to God. Where we still have places in our hearts that require more forgiveness. More healing. More love.

I don't know when or if or how broken relationships might be restored. I wonder if some will even happen in this broken garden or not until the next garden, the perfect one. Sometimes, my brain likes to make up stories to fill me with more expectations of what restoration and reunification are going to look like. Or when my miracles and mercies may take place. I guess that's the dreamer in me. The truth is I really don't know. I don't know what the ending of my Book of Life—or even what the next chapter—is going to look like. I'd love it if God would give me a little peek. I'd flip through a few pages to see what lies ahead. Just a little sneak. But He won't.

I think that would defeat our faith. And my faith tells me that our God restores! He loves me. And you. He knows our pain. More importantly, His promises are real.

There Is Beauty in the Pressure

I'm definitely a work in progress. Some days are tough, and some days I get to laugh and be silly. There are blessings in both. God sees the things I can't. He knows the things I don't know. And He knows I am only in the middle of my story. You and me both—we will have more hard moments to come, more triggers, and probably more pain. I'm sorry. The good news is we will also have some of the best moments of our lives too—if we allow them to come. Friend, one devastating life event is a lot to handle. So, when it seems like we are being continuously punched in the gut, it can become pretty exhausting. It's important to remember that we're just in the middle. We are still learning, growing, and healing. This is our way *through.* It's not over yet!

Building perseverance when we go through the hard things brings us to a place of building our character. It'll be a new character, one that will be better equipped to live out our divine purpose. God is molding us into who He wants us to be in this new chapter. And He does this in the middle.

Let's talk about two of my favorite things for a minute: diamonds and pearls. I know, girl cliché, right? I love them because they're pure and natural. God-made. Glorious and gorgeous. And they are my favorite color. But now, I have a new reason for loving them that I'm going to share with you.

Diamonds aren't diamonds at the beginning of their stories. Diamonds are carbon atoms bonding together at around 125 miles below the earth's surface. The pressure down there is about fifty thousand times the pressure of standing on land. They're heated at a temperature of approximately 2,900 degrees. (And we think Arizona summers are hot!) That's a whole lot of pressure, excessive heat, and crazy perseverance to become something so gorgeous at the end of their story. Talk about becoming new!

Diamonds represent love, commitment, purity, strength, good health, faithfulness, and eternity. Pretty excellent virtues, yeah?

And then there are pearls. They're formed from an irritant entering the shells of oysters and mussels. The mollusk responds to the irritant by slowly secreting layers of nacre, or mother-of-pearl, which is made of aragonite and conchiolin. These are the same materials that make up their shells. This process coats the irritant and protects the mollusk. Over time, the perseverance of many layers builds up to form a pearl. In the beginning, they're an irritant, and in the end, they're beautiful and glorious pearls.

Pearls represent love, devotion, purity, wisdom, resilience, determination, elegance, new beginnings, and perfection. Wow!

Sweet friend, we are going to face trials. We will have suffering and pain. We will experience extreme pressure and heat, and there will be irritants and triggers. There's no question: we are going to be tested for our faith. And in this, we will develop perseverance. We are becoming our own versions of diamonds and pearls. We will have the opportunity to share our beauty with others. We will get to be a testimony of God's healing power and goodness—not despite but *because of* the thorns we face . . .

> "I was given a thorn in my flesh, a messenger of Satan, to torment me. Three times I pleaded with the Lord to take it away from me. But he said to me, 'My grace is sufficient for you, for my power is made perfect in weakness.' Therefore I will boast all the more gladly about my weaknesses, so that Christ's power may rest on me. That is why, for Christ's sake, I delight in weaknesses, in insults, in hardships,

in persecutions, in difficulties. For when I am weak, then I am strong (2 Corinthians 12:7-10).

His Grace is sufficient for us. And His power is made perfect in our weakness, in the middle of our mess. Let Christ's power rest upon us. Let us not grow weary in our weakness, hardships, persecutions, and difficulties. For *when we are weak, then we are strong*. It is in these moments that we are facing pressure and irritation that we are becoming diamonds and pearls.

It's important when we find ourselves in the middle, after being knocked off-balance, that we refocus on our purpose. It's easy to lose sight of our purpose when we hit these bumps. Don't focus on the pain and suffering, the disappointment, the persecution, or any judgment. Don't let those things get ahold of your heart. Don't let them drag you back down into the pits of your Hell that you've fought so hard to get out of. Together, let us forget what is behind and press on to the big adventure ahead. "Remember Lot's wife," says Jesus.

As recorded, Jesus stood on the shore of the Sea of Tiberias while several of His disciples were out in the boat fishing (John 21:1-4). Well, they were trying to fish but were having an unsuccessful venture that night. Being not too far out from the land, they heard Jesus calling to them, but they couldn't tell who He was. They couldn't see Him. Remember, friend, just because we don't see Jesus or don't notice that it's Him, it doesn't mean He isn't there. He's always there. Jesus is with us right now. He was with us in our pain. He will be with us when an unexpected trigger knocks us off our feet. He always has been here. Just like He was for the disciples.

Divine Design for All

As a parent, there have been many times—too many to count—when I've gone to God in prayer and asked, begged, and pleaded with Him to protect my children from the hard things they were going through. I've prayed for Him to rescue them from their pain and grueling experiences. From suffering. One afternoon, while praying about this, God chose that time to pierce my heart. I heard Him whisper to me that there were things my kids would need to go through to become who He needed them to be. Wow!

I remind myself of this prayer moment often, usually when I want to protect them but can't—or shouldn't. I hurt for them when they make choices that hurt themselves. So, I'm grateful to share this truth with you today. When you're hurting for a loved one whose choices leave them in places or circumstances you wish they didn't have to endure, when you wish you could step in and protect them from the painful possibilities that lie ahead, remember two things: 1) God's got them and 2) there are lessons they need to learn to become who God wants them to be.

We are all living out our individual stories. God is leading us and guiding us and loving us through them all. And it's equally important to remember there are others in our lives who are living out their stories too—stories that will surely include God's direction, timing, and healing as well—because we are all His. He has a chapter in the Book of Life and a plan for us, collectively and individually.

The Fullness of a Grateful Heart

HARVESTING JOY

I have found in my healing journey that practicing gratitude and staying settled in a grateful heart help me catch my balance and become steady on my feet again. I try to stay in a mindset driven by gratitude as much as possible, thanking God for blessings throughout the day. Big or small. They all matter. Right now, I'm grateful for a fresh glass of water and a Perfect protein bar.

> **Practicing gratitude shifts our focus from ruminating on what we don't have to find joy in what we do have. There is always something to be grateful for.**

Practicing gratitude shifts our focus from ruminating on what we don't have to find joy in what we do have. There is always something to be grateful for.

Several years ago, I read a great book called *One Thousand Gifts* by Ann Voskamp. You should take a minute and put it in your Amazon cart. I read it twice and think I'll keep it in a regular reading rotation. While reading this book and for a long time afterward, I journaled blessings as they came into a cute little notebook set aside on my desk for just this purpose. These blessings became the focus of my sight, hearing, and awareness during this time. I did my best not to duplicate anything I was grateful for, although I am sure I did. This practice helped me turn my focus from all the suffering and sadness I was feeling to the tiny moments throughout the day in which I could find joy and be grateful. The little things in my daily story that I would usually take for granted. I found blessings even in the mundane—and especially in the super special.

In my blessing notebook, I always numbered them as I wrote them. Here are a few that I thought I'd share with you.

- 811. Crisp blue skies.
- 851. "I love you, Mama"

- 879. Rejuvenating Sundays.
- 949. Blessings bigger than I could have imagined.
- 967. Peace during something that used to trigger me.
- 975. Baby goat snuggles.
- 983. Perfectly timed books.
- 1023. Lunchtime hummingbird visits.
- 1052. Worship music filling the house.
- 1104. Long bike rides with Dylan.
- 1109. Boy 2 coming through the front door.
- 1115. My Tuesday morning girls.
- 1118. Sunshine through my office window.
- 1132. Warm melty chocolate in a freshly baked chocolate chip cookie.

Occasionally, I pull out that little notebook and write down something I'm certain is new. But most often, I just try to thank God right when I notice the blessing. It's become somewhat of a habit!

> "In every thing give thanks: for this is the will of God in Christ Jesus concerning you" (1 Thessalonians 5:18, KJV).

Yes! Let us give thanks in all circumstances. I'm not saying you should give thanks for the things that are hurting you, but you can. You might be to that place in your healing, and if you are, you're a total rock star in my book! You can give me tips. But if you're like me and not in that place yet, we can still find gratitude and thanksgiving for something else in the middle of the hard thing, like safety or health. Or that God is with us and we can feel His presence. We can learn to embrace *something* in the moment.

Friend, I want you to know that I'm sorry for all that you've been through. I know you've been hurting. And I may not have suffered the same hurts, but please know you're not alone.

Remember when Jesus walked on water and called Simon (Peter) to come out to Him? As long as Simon kept his eyes on Jesus, his focus steady on the only thing that could keep him steady, Simon remained on top of the water. But as soon as he took his eyes off Jesus, he sank. The same happens with us. We need to remember who will keep us from sinking into the depths of our disappointments. Though we flail when turbulent waters come our way, Jesus will anchor us. He will lift us out of the storm, but we must fix our eyes on Him. We must reach for Him. Let him take our hand and take hold of His lead.

This is our season for finding joy in what is and finding things to be grateful for, even when we're hit with painful circumstances or unexpected trigger moments. When our moment of happiness suddenly gets knocked off-balance, let us turn our hearts from pain and suffering to healing and gratitude. Especially for how far we've already come. This garden isn't for the faint of heart.

Let us become the glorious and beautiful diamonds and pearls the master creator is developing us into. Through the flames. Through the heat. Through the pressure. Let us find perseverance to become all that He desires us to be. Because, friend, it's not over yet.

Chapter Twelve

Naked and Afraid

It's been years since I've entered this place. I still long for happy Christmases together in our not-matching Christmas jammies, eating peppermint ice cream, with the lights off and the room aglow with the beautiful soft glimmer of the lights on our giant tree. I want a family movie night with homemade popcorn—salty, with a little too much butter. I want to buy the special thing I see in a store and give the perfect gift for no reason other than I just know someone is going to love it. I want what was taken. Stolen. I want calm and peace. My biggest desire is to hold my children and grandchildren until I'm whole. Then I remember Christ makes me whole.

As I kneel before God in prayer. It's my natural behavior to bow my head. Maybe it's the gravitational pull. Maybe it's reverence. Either way, I bow before the Father. On my knees, hands folded and resting in my lap, I am in the posture of complete submission. I'm not sure this is how it's supposed to be, but this position seems to be how I naturally settle in for my alone time with Him.

Often, though, without even considering what's happening, my chin lifts, and my face turns upward toward Him. I surrender to the Spirit. But recently, I've been feeling that He's telling me He is the One lifting my chin toward Him. Just as any loving father would when we are sad and hurting or need to tell us something really important. He's lifting my chin so I may see the love and compassion in His eyes. When life's disappointments are too much, when I feel weak and insecure, He lifts my chin to look to Him. It's part of His healing. His praise. His love. His view of who I am seeps into my soul in those moments. I haven't really paid attention to this in the past. And now that God's bringing my awareness to it, I'm noticing it happens quite regularly. And I feel even more loved in this realization.

As my chin raises and my face turns to Him, the light shines brightly upon me. Warm and peaceful, just like His love. I am grateful for this new in*sight*. And now that I recognize it is happening, I smile because I know it's Him.

But there are moments when my chin is lifted, and tears still stream down my cheeks. They're not always sad, broken tears. Often, they're happy, grateful, joyful, and blessed tears. Because even though I'm still in the middle, I'm still between perfect gardens, and I am blessed. I am taken care of. I am wanted. I am enough. I have much to be grateful for.

And so do you!

Seasons of suffering are not for nothing. We are not defined by our past or our circumstances. And we are not defined by our rejection from others. We are not defined by the opinions of others. We have been accepted by the beloved, and no rejection from others changes that.

"As you come to him, the living Stone—rejected by humans but chosen by God and precious to him—" (1 Peter 2:4).

"The LORD is close to the brokenhearted and saves those who are crushed in spirit. The righteous person may have many troubles, but the LORD delivers him from them all" (Psalm 34:18-19).

"'For I know the plans I have for you,' declares the LORD, 'plans to prosper you and not to harm you, plans to give you hope and a future. Then you will call on me and come and pray to me,

> and I will listen to you. You will seek me and find me when you seek me with all your heart. I will be found by you,' declares the LORD, 'and will bring you back from captivity. I will gather you from all the nations and places where I have banished you,' declares the LORD, 'and will bring you back to the place from which I carried you into exile'" (Jeremiah 29:11-14).

At some point in our lives, we will experience loss. Perhaps multiple times. We feel the pain and suffering from all kinds of challenging life events. Whether it's grieving the loss of a loved one after death or the loss of someone through divorce or life choices — or by being taken away — we will feel the loss of dreams and hopes. Loss may also come in the form of a job or home or other possessions. And we can even feel the loss of self that can come from all of those many different circumstances. Loss is all around us. But we can still live well.

> "Heal me, O LORD, and I shall be healed; save me, and I shall be saved: for thou art my praise"
> (Jeremiah 17:14, KJV).

The Essential Role of Vulnerability in Healing

In our healing journeys, we will pass through many stages. From my experience, there are seven of them. Some are akin to those of the official grief cycle. I call them awareness, acknowledgment, acceptance, feeling, grieving, forgiveness, and moving forward. Most of these will unfold in no particular order; however, I'm pretty sure moving forward is the last stage. We have covered all of these at some point in our journey together throughout these pages, but I wanted to take a moment and talk about them here because I feel like in each of these steps, there is a huge amount of vulnerability to achieve.

The healing journey will require you to have the courage to be vulnerable to yourself and others — and God. I think a large part of that vulnerability includes listening to the Holy Spirit. We will be placed into situations and circumstances that will push us, possibly to our limits and beyond. Healing is not for the faint of heart. It is not the easy way out. The easy way out is not really a way out. It's getting stuck. When you choose not to do the healing, you're most likely choosing to bury the pain. Bury the memories. Pretend like the hurt and life-changing moments didn't happen. You're pretending, and that's just living a lie. Please don't bury anything.

You can be brave and do the work. Your loved ones need you. You need you. The world needs you. I need you.

Vulnerability needs awareness. This includes being brave enough to identify and recognize your feelings in and around the trauma you've endured. And in doing so, you will know what areas you need to work on. That's where the triggers become a blessing. They help you understand where you need to do the work. When you're at the beginning of your healing journey, you may need to make a list of what comes up because you can't process and heal them all in one sit-down session with God and yourself. This takes time. Have a quiet moment and ask yourself the hard questions. Ask yourself what you're feeling about the trauma. What feelings come up? Shock, fear, anger, anxiety, helplessness, withdrawal? Later in your healing, you can tackle those triggers as they come.

Vulnerability is an acknowledgment. It's an acceptance that the trauma happened and is a part of your story. Sometimes, this will include admitting your faults or the part you played in the event. Sometimes, it's realizing there's nothing more you can do to make the situation any different. But most importantly, it's acknowledging that you have healing to do and that it's up to you to do it. It's you who has to choose to heal. It's you who has to choose to do the hard parts. Nobody can do the work for you.

Vulnerability in acceptance. This looks like admitting that *this* is where you are. The big, scary thing happened. The dust settled, and something else is your new normal. This is what it is. You can't go back. You can't change what was done. Accepting that healing is going to take whatever time it takes. Giving yourself love, grace, and patience in your journey and committing yourself to do the work tells you that you're worth it. You can do it!

Honor vulnerability with your feelings. You must feel all the things you're feeling. Please don't skip this step. You have to feel your emotions. You cannot go numb, bury them, or make the big, scary thing go away. Part of the healing is the feeling. It's going to suck. It's going to hurt like mad. It's going to make you exhausted and weak. Angry. Sad. All the things. I know. But please be vulnerable with yourself and God and feel it all. You have to feel it to move through it. Be patient with and kind to yourself. Include things you love to do or that bring you peace (i.e., self-care) during this time. Love on yourself. For me, that means a hot bath with a book or a quiet hike, talking to God. Often, I just crave quiet time alone. As you engage with yourself, remember to speak lovingly to yourself.

Vulnerability in grieving. This looks like grieving the trauma itself but also grieving the unmet expectations, the "what should have beens." I was a long time into my healing journey when I realized I had been grieving the loss and trauma but not the "what should have beens." Think of it this way: if your loss includes the death of a loved one, there is typically a funeral or memorial service. Those events permit us to grieve. What if we gave ourselves permission to grieve the other losses the same way? What if we had a funeral for our traumas? A funeral for the "what should have beens?" A funeral for the job loss or the loss of a friendship. What might that look like?

Friend, please give yourself time to grieve. There is no specific time frame. Don't hurry it. However, it is important to not get stuck here.

Vulnerability in forgiveness. We are taught that we need to forgive as Jesus forgave. There is a vulnerability in forgiving. Sometimes, we may feel like it's our right to hold on to the thing that hurts us. To keep blaming someone else for the event and the pain. But in addition to forgiving others, I also feel there's a beautiful vulnerability in forgiving yourself for the part you played. I know so many who struggle with this. Maybe that's your most vulnerable part of forgiveness? Or maybe it's forgiving God? We must be brave enough to let go of the blame, anger, resentment, and hostility toward others, ourselves, and God. Ask Him to help you; He will.

Vulnerability in moving forward. Phew! This is big because when we've been through something that rocks our world, we are no longer who we used to be. Maybe the vulnerability is in admitting that we are not the same person who we were before the big, scary thing crushed us to dust. Being vulnerable to the idea of becoming a new creation may seem daunting. But actually doing it—that's huge! Being vulnerable in this area includes committing to yourself and God that you're ready to have a new outlook. You're ready for a new life that doesn't include festering in pain and suffering. Ready for a new purpose. A new direction. A new identity. You'll be creating your new future and taking steps to make those new goals and dreams a reality. Being vulnerable in moving forward may look like a move, a new job, a new workout routine, or a new hobby. It may look like volunteering or making new friends. It may be a new haircut or taking a trip by yourself. The most important part is that you're brave in this step. You deserve to smile and be happy! You deserve to be healed and whole. You deserve to live life thriving and not just surviving.

My friend, you are reading the work of my vulnerability. But God didn't drop me here into the deep end of the pool and expect me to swim without knowing how. He let me get into the pool one step at a time and then stand on my tippy toes as I approached the deep end. Vulnerability has been my struggle. But our Father in Heaven is so faithful. He didn't let me stay there in the dark, shallow life I was experiencing all alone. He didn't want me hiding under my desk, either. He has given me small opportunities to be vulnerable in my healing so that this book He has asked me to write wasn't so huge. It came to be one small, vulnerable step at a time.

The Courage to Heal

I struggled with vulnerability in my trauma, especially at the beginning, because I had no idea what was going on. I was ashamed. I wondered what people would think of me if they knew what I was going through. Would people judge me?

But one day, I chose to be brave. One day, I shared a little bit of my story. On this day, God gave me the courage to speak out. And when I did, guess what happened? None of the fears I gripped happened. Not one question I feared answering came up. Not one pointed accusation crept in. Those were all just part of the package the enemy used to keep me silent, afraid, and not sharing or helping others.

What I did get were messages and comments from others who were experiencing or knew families who were experiencing the same loss of children through parental alienation and similar false accusations, legal battles, court system shenanigans, and horror I had been too ashamed to share. In my vulnerability and sharing, I got to help people become aware of this kind of trauma. I got to share what parental alienation is and what to watch out for so that others would recognize the alienating tactics and take a stand to help their families.

And since then, I've had parents reach out to me in desperation because alienation was happening to them. God is using my vulnerability to help save children. To help protect them from losing a parent they love and desperately need to be with. To be a light in the darkness that other parents in their own desperation and darkness need.

> "You can't help anyone if you don't share your story."

One season, I prayed God would show me how He wanted me to use this experience that I'd been living to help others. Plain as day, He said to my spirit, "You can't help anyone if you don't share your story." And there you have it. He called me out of hiding on that day—and in many more moments since.

Since that call to vulnerability, I've been in several situations that have allowed me to be even more vulnerable. God is giving me practice. Remember how I shared that God had led me to several community groups and the beautiful women who had since become dear friends? They all came after the trauma. *After* my life changed forever. So, none of them saw me walk the tortuous path.

One of my ladies' groups does a monthly hike when it's not superhot. I was new to the group, and this must've been the second or third hike I had attended. When I arrived, the only other woman there was the woman who ran the group. I was excited about the one-on-one time with her to get to know her better. During this hike, I felt the Holy Spirit prompt me to share some of my story with her. As we hiked and talked and shared deep moments of our individual stories with each other, I learned in this intimate time on the mountain, with God ever-present, that I was, in fact, safe. That no judgment or persecution came with the sharing of myself or the story I had been too ashamed to talk about. There was only love, support, and safety.

In another vulnerable moment in the middle of processing and healing, a new trigger moment came. I love to hike and be on the mountaintop with God and had been going pretty regularly during this time. When I go hiking, my doodle is always with me, and he drinks a lot of water, so I carry a pack with plenty of water for both of us. I don't know if it was the weight of the pack or the sweat of the warm desert hikes, but I was getting some bumps on my shoulders and back. My husband noticed them as I stripped down to shower the sweat and dust away.

Panic hit me when he followed me to the shower to scrub the bumps with my favorite body scrub. I don't know about you, but standing naked in the full light of day as my husband scrubbed my back was a completely vulnerable moment for me. I was already emotional and feeling weak and worn out from the hike, and then this fully bare vulnerability just topped it all off. He was serving me and loving me—taking care of me with no expectations. Nothing was required in return. He was just serving in love. I don't think he even noticed how hard this moment was for me. Or the tears that flowed as I showered afterward all alone. But his love for me at that moment was exactly what I needed.

These vulnerable moments in our healing journey are huge blessings. They show us that Satan is a liar. The truth is we are so very loved by a good God. There are so many people already in our lives ready to lift us and love on us. Friend, I encourage you to step into the vulnerable moments, one God-guided step at a time. Let Him show you the blessings in those moments. Let Him show you that you are safe and cherished. You are good enough. Those around you want to hear your story and your testimony. They will benefit from seeing your tears and journeying with you.

> *"'Peace, peace, to those far and near,' says the LORD. 'And I will heal them'"* (Isaiah 57:19).

It is my prayer that you will find peace in your vulnerability and your healing journey. You are not alone. Jesus is there with you, every step. Lean into Him. Be brave and commit to one step at a time. I cannot wait to see what God does in your story!

Chapter Thirteen

Sound the Trumpets!

As God called me to write this "love letter" to you, I felt a special word settle into my heart.

While in prayer, I was brimming with curiosity and hope for the future. I was looking forward to a season of quiet reflection and healing from all the loss (e.g., children, property, health). And with excited anticipation, I watched to see what God had planned for Dylan and me, for our family.

As I prayed, I felt the gentle whisper of one word: *jubilee*. I couldn't shake it. This beautiful and interesting word seeped into my soul. I didn't know what the word really meant or how it would weave into where I was in this new chapter—or into any chapter to come. I just knew I was receiving this word for this new season. And I knew I needed to dive deep into Scripture to learn what God wanted me to receive. I also knew right away that I was to share this word and the message behind it with you right here, dear friend.

Jubilee: the year of the Lord's Favor. This is a year marked by the remission of sins, the cancellation of debts, and a general pardon. The book of Leviticus explains a jubilee year occurred every fifty years, during which slaves and prisoners were released, debts were forgiven, and God's mercies were especially evident.

Whether you've only been in this messy middle for a minute or you've been here for a long while. Your jubilee is ready and waiting for you too! Right now. I believe it in my heart.

> Whether you've only been in this messy middle for a minute or you've been here for a long while. Your jubilee is ready and waiting for you too! Right now.

We first see the word *jubilee* in Leviticus 25. It was part of the Law that God gave the Israelites, called the Year of Jubilee (Leviticus 25:10–11). In these verses, God tells the Israelites they should take part in a special "resetting." The people are called to rest, and those in slavery are set free. (I'm thinking of emotional slavery as well.) Debts are forgiven (and not just the monetary ones). It is a time of restoration and renewal and a time to come home. A season of celebration. The whole idea is for a reset to reestablish good relationships with God and one another.

The Hebrew word for *jubilee* comes from the word *yobel*. The literal translation is "ram's horn." This ram's horn is the Israelites' trumpet. And the sound of the ram's horn is the signaling of the beginning of the Year of Jubilee. So, let's sound the trumpets! This is the beginning of our jubilee! I don't know about you, but I'm ready for a season of celebration.

Jubilee is our rest. We mustn't forget this very important part: We are to rest our minds, our bodies, and our souls. Rest from our work. Rest from our healing and our emotions. Rest in His presence. Our jubilee is our Sabbath reminder. God calls us to rest as He rested. Our rest is where we reconnect with God, rest in Him, and renew our spirits.

Jubilee is our reset. We can start new. Our fresh start is now. And again tomorrow. Then next week. We don't need to wait for any particular event or time to begin again. We can step out and into our new chapter starting now. There's no waiting to receive our Year of Jubilee or our new beginning. We don't need to wait to receive our restoration or our coming home.

Jubilee is our forgiveness. It's time to forgive others, especially those who don't offer us an apology. We must also forgive ourselves and God (not because He did anything wrong but because it helps us let go of our bitterness). Let us step into forgiveness right now. Let's not wait another minute. Through the blood of Jesus, our Father has already forgiven us. Receive this truth now! In our jubilee, we can wrap ourselves in total forgiveness and receive the peace waiting for us on the inside of God's grace.

Jubilee is freedom. Let us step into the freedom God is waiting for us to receive. In Him, we are free indeed (John 8:36). We can receive Christ's freedom and find pure joy in God and all the blessings that surround us each moment of every single day. We can break the shackles of fear, anger, betrayal, or distrust that have held us in captivity and receive our freedom now.

Jubilee is restoration. God can restore all that was lost as He intends. There's restoration of our health, smiles, peace, and joy. And all the other things we hope for. Remember, don't hold on to the idea that this means everything will be restored to the way it was because it doesn't. We don't belong in the past. God is moving us forward into something new. Be open to God's plan. It's so much better than ours!

Jubilee is renewal. This is our "all things new"—a renewal of health, finances, relationships, and everything else taken from us. This is becoming who God is calling us to become and doing what He is calling us to do. This is where we see Him putting us back together better than before. This is where we shine, out in the open, for the entire world to see. This is where we show everyone we didn't let the enemy keep us down. This is where our identity is renewed in truth, for we belong to the King!

Jesus said, "The Spirit of the Lord is on me, because he has anointed me to proclaim good news to the poor. He has sent me to proclaim freedom for the prisoners and recovery of sight for the blind, to set the oppressed free, to proclaim the year of the Lord's favor" (Luke 4:18–19). (The year of the Lord's favor is *Jubilee*.)

> *"Today this scripture is fulfilled in your hearing"* (Luke 4:21).

Don't miss this! The year of the Lord's favor is Jubilee!!! And it is fulfilled in your hearing. The Good News is here. *Now.* You are no longer a prisoner of your past. You are free! You are no longer blinded by the awful pain and suffering that you've endured. Your sight is restored. You are no longer oppressed and powerless. You are strong!

Sound the trumpets! Jesus is our Jubilee! And this is our celebration!

In the Gospel of Luke, Jesus declares He is the one foretold by the prophet Isaiah in Isaiah 61. Jesus is the Messiah and the fulfillment of Jubilee! Not every fifty years, but today!!! Right now.

> *"Jesus is the fulfillment of Jubilee."*

The life, death, and resurrection of Jesus is our reset. Because of all that He is and all that He has done, Jesus is our Jubilee. Jesus is our foundation of hope and the promise of our future. He ushers in the new creation we have been promised, and we can receive all that was lost. Jesus made a way for all of these blessings to be available to us. And our new beginning can start right now! Now is the day of salvation (2 Corinthians 6:2).

You have been hurting long enough, friend. You have endured enough suffering. Sin. Persecution. Judgment. Sorrow and pain. You have been depressed and lonely for long enough. You do not have to wait for your Jubilee to come because it's right now! The time has come to claim your victory in Jesus.

Friend, let us go to God in prayer and ask for Him for our Jubilee. Ask that our Father in Heaven restore all that has been lost. We can ask for whatever the devil has stolen to be returned to us as He did with Job. We can ask God to heal all of our broken places. Ask Him to help us heal from our grief and restore our joy. The time is now! Let's lay it all at His feet and let Him restore us.

Remember, God calls us:

- Loved (1 John 4:10).
- Beautiful (Song of Solomon 4:7).
- Chosen (1 Thessalonians 1:4).
- Forgiven (1 John 1:9).
- A new creation (2 Corinthians 5:17).

- Blessed (Galatians 3:9).
- Victorious (Revelation 12:11).
- Set free (John 8:32).
- Strong (Philippians 4:13).
- Healed (1 Peter 2:24).
- Alive (Ephesians 2:4–5).
- Reconciled (2 Corinthians 5:18).
- More than a conqueror (Romans 8:37).
- Complete (Colossians 2:10).

The purpose of your Jubilee is to release all of your past hurts, debts, burdens, and unforgiveness to God, who is our ultimate provider. Let Him restore you. He loves you too much to let you stay in suffering. You are free. Forgiven. Release all that has bound you. Held you down. Anchored you in captivity. Your debts are forgiven through the blood of Jesus, and the time is now to receive your Jubilee!

> "Behold, I will do a new thing" (Isaiah 43:19, KJV).

> "Instead of your shame you will receive a double portion, and instead of disgrace

> *you will rejoice in your inheritance. And so you will inherit a double portion in your land, and everlasting joy will be yours"* (Isaiah 61:7).

And when He heals you and blesses you, when He brings you through the flames and delivers you into Jubilee, you will shout His praise and let everyone know Who did it! When He pours out His double portion of grace and love upon you, shout His praise! When He returns the air to your lungs and the smile to your beautiful face, dance and worship for all to see!

Afterword

Shawna is a light on a hill that cannot be hidden. Through all the enemy has thrown at her in an attempt to keep her from sharing her message, her light continues to shine brightly.

I work with patients on a weekly basis who are children with alienated parents. They have and do suffer greatly. Though I work with the opposite side of the equation, I hear the pain, anguish, and trauma that this broken relationship brings. When a parent does not get the opportunity to disciple their child and does not have the opportunity to love them and model God's love, when a parent is made or becomes an enemy, suffering ensues.

Some of the greatest symptoms of parental alienation are abandonment and loneliness. Children struggle to understand why this is happening in their family, why they have been chosen to suffer, and why their family cannot just be "normal." The lies about their worth and calling run deep. They often turn to substances or unhealthy relationships to fill the void.

Shawna has stepped out in incredible courage against these lies. She stands in the gap, allowing others to know they aren't the only ones. Her beautiful vulnerability and honesty allow others in similar circumstances to feel seen, known, and heard.

In choosing to write and share about her personal story, she also allows children who have chosen or been told to alienate their parents what it feels like to be on the other side. How what they have been told or believe to be "truth" may not be so.

Anytime we stand in the gap, anytime we fight against lies and darkness, anytime we show up in full vulnerability and love to promote healing for others, we wage war against an enemy, who is very real. Shawna has fought the darkness in her life and now brings her light to fight for others.

It is an honor to know her and to know her story; her light is truly contagious. I pray you have been able to heal a bit reading her story and can move forward with new-found confidence that you are not alone. To know that there *is* a fourth man in the fire with you.

Keep fighting the darkness, friends. The power of family and the power that love holds will always be victorious. Our Jesus has defeated the darkness once and for all. May all families be healed and restored in His name.

In Jesus's unconditional love,

Pamela Snyder, Master Parenting Coach and Certified Family Trauma Specialist

About the Author

Shawna Foster is a vibrant Christ-follower, devoted wife, and loving mother whose sunny disposition infuses every endeavor she undertakes. As a dedicated realtor in beautiful Phoenix, Arizona, Shawna possesses a natural talent for connecting with people, highlighted by her appearance on a North Phoenix episode of *My Lottery Dream Home*.

Shawna has survived the brokenness, pain, rejection, betrayal, persecution, and judgment often associated with the heart-wrenching experience of losing a child. Through her journey, she has discovered forgiveness, hope, and healing, and she is passionate about sharing these gifts with others.

Shawna has a heart for service, having previously dedicated her time to working with children, in women's ministry, and building homes for single mothers. Currently, she serves at The Phoenix Dream Center, where she mentors young women rescued from sex trafficking. Additionally, she plays a vital role on the fundraising board for Stop Traffic Walk, helping to combat this critical issue. Shawna also serves on the Board of Directors for Moment 2 Moment

Ministries—empowering families of special needs children with support, resources, and community.

Living in the Valley of the Sun with her husband Dylan and their adorable doodle, Shawna finds joy in outdoor adventures, including hiking and mountain biking beneath the breathtaking Arizona sky. A passionate traveler, she cherishes making unforgettable memories with her loved ones.

My Gift To You—
a collection of songs to encourage your soul, deepen your faith, and journey with you into renewal.

Immerse yourself in music that uplifts, inspires, and accompanies you on your journey of restoration and purpose. I've curated a special Spotify playlist filled with powerful Christian songs that speak to my heart. Download this free playlist now and let these songs remind you of God's presence, His love, and the hope, joy, and strength waiting for you each day.

Shawna Marie Foster

Reflect and Heal: Moving Beyond the Pain

Download my free journaling prompts and start writing your way out of the past and into a restored, purposeful life.

Your story doesn't end with the trauma—it's where healing and transformation begin. I've created a set of Reflective Journaling Prompts to help you process your "before and after" moments, guiding you to reflect and step into the healing and hope God has for you.

Shawna Marie Foster

Connect with Shawna!

friend + follow

Tune in to Faith in the Flames Podcast: Transforming Trauma Into Hope and Healing!

Come with Shawna as she walks alongside women moving from brokenness to wholeness through faith, resilience, and love. This isn't a place to re-live pain but a space to embrace healing, joy, and the beautiful purpose God has for you! Available on most streaming platforms.

F. I.T.
PRESS

Your story doesn't just matter for you, it matters to move others!

1 CHRONICLES 16:24 (NLT)
Publish His glorious deeds among the nations. Tell everyone about the amazing things he does.

A Christian Publishing House dedicated to turning messages into movements. On mission to mobilize the critical voices for such a time as this. Specializing in co-hort compilations, to make way for writers to collaborate with other prolific members of the Body of Christ. Our works open conversations around mental, physical, relational, financial and spiritual health and wholeness journeys, often directly associated to our rooted identity and purpose driven life.

Learn More & Don't Wait to Get Published!

www.ingramcontent.com/pod-product-compliance
Lightning Source LLC
Chambersburg PA
CBHW060601080526
44585CB00013B/648